WATERSIDE WALKS
in
The Chilterns

D1643359

Jean Patefield

COUNTRYSIDE BOOKS
Newbury, Berkshire

First published 2008
© Jean Patefield, 2008

COUNTRYSIDE BOOKS
3 Catherine Road
Newbury, Berkshire

To view our complete range of books,
please visit us at
www.countrysidebooks.co.uk

ISBN 978 1 84674 077 0

Designed by Peter Davies
Produced through MRM Associates Ltd., Reading
Printed in Thailand

All material for the manufacture of this book
was sourced from sustainable forests

Contents

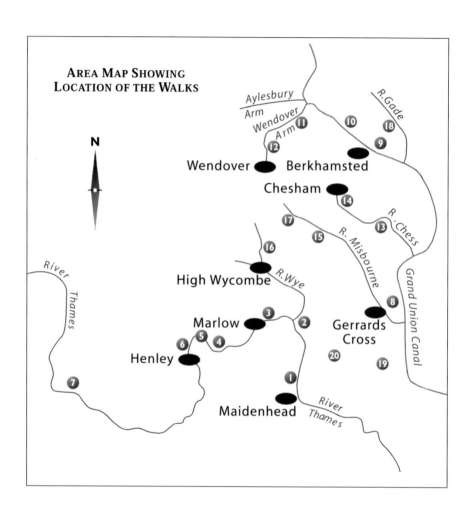

AREA MAP SHOWING
LOCATION OF THE WALKS

Walk

PUBLISHER'S NOTE

We hope that you obtain considerable enjoyment from this book; great care has been taken in its preparation. Although at the time of publication all routes followed public rights of way or permitted paths, diversion orders can be made and permissions withdrawn.

We cannot, of course, be held responsible for such diversion orders and any inaccuracies in the text which result from these or any other changes to the routes nor any damage which might result from walkers trespassing on private property. We are anxious though that all details covering the walks are kept up to date and would therefore welcome information from readers which would be relevant to future editions.

The simple sketch maps that accompany the walks in this book are based on notes made by the author whilst checking the routes on the ground. They are designed to show you how to reach the start and to point out the main features of the overall circuit, and they contain a progression of numbers that relate to the paragraphs of the text.

However, for the benefit of a proper map, we do recommend that you purchase the relevant Ordnance Survey sheet covering your walk. The Ordnance Survey maps are widely available, especially through booksellers and local newsagents.

INTRODUCTION

The Chilterns are an arc of chalk hills about 40 miles north and west of London, stretching through Berkshire, Oxfordshire, Buckinghamshire, and Hertfordshire. The hills are essentially made of chalk; indeed the word Chiltern comes from the Saxon word for chalk. Chalk is a very porous rock and water drains through it rapidly. Therefore the Chilterns are very dry, with little running water; so a book of waterside walks might seem an unlikely proposition. However, there are significant waterways and the walks in this book divide into three, more or less equal groups.

The southern boundary is universally agreed to be one of England's great rivers, the Thames, and seven walks explore sections of the river from Cliveden and Maidenhead in the east (walk 1) to Goring in the west (walk 7). Passage along the river itself has been a right since Magna Carta, but the towpath did not exist until the Thames Commissioners were appointed in the 18th century. One of their roles was to make and maintain a towpath but this was no easy task. The land bordering the river was in private hands and there were many natural barriers such as swamps. This means that the riverside path is sometimes on the north bank and sometimes on the south, as was expedient at the time. People and horses were carried from one side to the other by numerous ferries, and every Thamesside community of any age has a Ferry Lane. Sadly, the ferries have all now gone and their demise often makes crossing the river difficult for pedestrians, mostly confining walks to one bank or the other.

At both Goring and Cliveden the Thames has broken through the chalk and there are magnificent cliffs overlooking the river.

Five routes explore the second great but man-made waterway of the Chilterns. The Grand Union Canal is a feat of late 18th-century engineering. It passes through Tring Gap, which has always been a natural route through the Chilterns and so has attracted monumental engineering works from the Romans onwards. The canal was originally called the Grand Junction Canal and was part of a scheme to link the Trent with the Thames so that coal and other cargoes could be transported economically to London from the Midlands and the North. It was built by William Jessop, who constructed a series of locks to take boats up to 430 ft at Tring summit and down the other side.

Every time lock gates are opened some water is lost, but in the dry Chilterns there are few natural sources for replenishment. The

The River Thames seen from Bourne End bridge on Walk 2

Wendover arm (walk 12) was built to collect water from the springs at the base of the Chilterns and was upgraded to become navigable. Almost as soon as the canal was opened to Tring summit it became clear that these water supplies were inadequate, and it quickly became clear that the Wendover arm was leaking badly and even draining water from the canal. The solution was to build a number of reservoirs near Tring (walk 11) from which water could be pumped up into the canal. Even with these, water was always a problem and a borehole was sunk at Cow Roast (walk 10) in the drought of 1902, which remains in use to this day.

The canal was a busy commercial waterway until the coming of the railways. There is now negligible commercial traffic and the canal is given over to pleasure boats.

The third category, of six walks, explores the rivers of the Chilterns. Much of the charm of the Chiltern landscape comes from the valleys, locally called bottoms, but they are nearly all dry, and the rivers that do exist are small, pathetic things compared with rivers in areas of less permeable geology. The valleys were formed in the Ice Age. The Chilterns were not covered by ice but were frozen much of the time. During the short sub-arctic summers water flowed from the glaciers only a short distance north and eroded the valleys we see today.

The rivers are small specimens for two reasons. Firstly, they flow only when the water table in the underlying chalk is high enough for the water to reach the surface. This is more likely in winter, and so the rivers are called winterbournes. Therefore, it is possible that you may do one of these routes and it will not be a waterside walk at all! However, go back after a wet spell and the water will have re-appeared.

Historical records suggest that at least some of the Chilterns' rivers, notably the Bulbourne (walks 9 and 10) and the Misbourne (walks 15 and 17), were more substantial in the past. The second reason they are less reliable than they used to be is over-abstraction of ground water from the underlying chalk aquifer. This has been particularly scandalous in the case of the Misbourne. The problem has now been recognized and measures introduced to try and alleviate the situation, and I am glad to say these seem to be having some effect.

Please do not let the capricious nature of the Chiltern rivers put you off these circuits. Some of the Chilterns' rivers usually flow well, notably the Chess (walks 13 and 14), the Gade (walk 18), the Wye (walk 2), and Hughenden stream (walk 16). The routes explore some of the best walking country in the south of England and the rivers are very pretty when they are in flow. Within the 400 square miles encompassed by the Chilterns are about 1,500 miles of public footpaths, mostly very quiet, well signed, and lovingly maintained. One walk (5) offers the chance to compare the might of the Thames with the small stream in the incomparable Hambleden valley.

If the Chilterns were just chalk they would resemble the other areas of chalk upland in southern England. However, the tops of the Chilterns are overlaid in many places with clay, which is much less permeable to water and supports quite different flora and fauna. This causes the phenomenon of swilly holes, explored on walk 20 in the beautiful Burnham Beeches.

Water adds immeasurably to the landscape, and vistas from stately homes often include a man-made lake, as on walks 8, 15, and 17, as well as, in particular, the two lakes explored on walk 19. Attractive lakes have also formed where gravel has been extracted and the abandoned workings have flooded (walks 3 and 8).

The twenty walks in this book are all between 2½ and 7½ miles long and should be well within the capacity of the average person, including those of mature years and families with children. They are intended to take the walker through this attractive corner of England at a gentle pace, with plenty of time to stop and stare, to savour the beauty and interest all around. A dedicated yomper and stomper could probably knock off the whole book in a single weekend but in doing so they would have missed the point and seen nothing. To fully appreciate the countryside it is necessary to go slowly with your eyes and ears open.

Some of the walks are short and level, ideal for a pipe opener on a winter's day, or giving plenty of time to dawdle away a summer's afternoon. Others are longer or more strenuous, some making an excellent all-day expedition. Several of the walks involve some climbing. This is inevitable, as the hills add enormous interest and with no ascents there are no views. However, this presents no problem to the sensible walker, who has three uphill gears – slowly, very slowly, and admiring the view.

All the routes are on public rights of way or permissive paths and have been carefully checked but, of course, in the countryside things do change. In particular, there is a welcome trend in the Chilterns towards replacing stiles with gates. These are easier to navigate, especially with a dog, and less prone to becoming hazardous.

A sketch map illustrates each walk, and they are all circular. An Ordnance Survey map is useful as well, especially for identifying the main features of views. The Explorer 1:25,000 (2½ inches to 1 mile) series are by far the best maps to use for walking. Sheets 171, 172, 181, and 182 cover the walks in this book. The grid reference of the starting point and the appropriate maps are given for each walk.

The walks all start where a car can be conveniently left, and directions to the starting points are given, together with some indication of the refreshments available along the way. Some of the routes, especially walks 2, 7, 8, 9, 14, and 17, can easily be accessed by rail.

So, put on your walking shoes and prepare to be delighted by the charms of that rarity – a waterside walk in the Chilterns.

Jean Patefield

9

COOKHAM AND CLIVEDEN REACH

The highlight of this easy walk is Cliveden Reach, where the river hugs the base of steep chalk cliffs thickly clad with magnificent trees. Many consider this to be the most beautiful stretch of the Thames. Starting at once-fashionable Boulters Lock, down river of Cliveden Reach, the route soon leaves the confines of Maidenhead behind and follows a stream-side path across fields to the pretty village of Cookham. There we pick up the Thames Path, which soon leads to the river and a walk beside Cliveden Reach back to Boulters Lock.

The river at point 8 of the walk

- **DISTANCE:** 6 miles
- **MAP:** OS Explorer 172 Chiltern Hills East
- **STARTING POINT:** Boulters Lock car park, Maidenhead: GR 902828
- **HOW TO GET THERE:** The car park is on the west side of the A4094 Maidenhead–Bourne End road, about a mile north of its junction with the A4 at Maidenhead Bridge.
- **REFRESHMENTS:** The Crown (tel. 01628 520163) in Cookham is well placed about halfway round the walk and serves food. There are also other pubs in Cookham.

THE WALK

1. Take a path at the left rear of the car park through to a road. Turn left. At a T-junction turn right. Some 15 yards after a road called The Pagoda, turn right on a fenced path. At the end of the path continue ahead on Summerleaze Road, passing Summerleaze Lake on the left.

2. When Summerleaze Road bends left and becomes Blackamoor Lane, take the left-hand one of two paths ahead, soon passing through a squeeze barrier and kissing gate, to a second kissing gate and cross-track.

3. Turn right. When the track ends continue ahead along the right-hand side of a common. At the end bear right to a drive. Cross the drive and go ahead to a footbridge.

4. Over the bridge turn left beside a stream, not straying onto a surfaced cycleway. Carry on by the stream when the path joins the surfaced cycleway, signed 'Green Way West', and press on in the same direction when the cycleway turns left after 50 yards. Cross a track and keep by the stream to a second track.

From this path there is an excellent view of Cliveden perched on the cliffs above the Thames. Cliveden has had many owners, and the house has been destroyed and rebuilt twice. The first house was built by George Villiers, 2nd Duke of Buckingham, who acquired the estate soon after the Restoration. He also laid out gardens and planted beech woods on what had been barren chalk cliffs above the Thames. The house was burned down in 1795 and remained derelict for several years. It was rebuilt in 1824 and then destroyed by fire again in 1849. The present house was built in 1850-51. From 1893 it was the home of the Astor family, who gave it to the National Trust in 1942. They lived in the house until 1966 and it is now used as a hotel.

However, it must be admitted that Cliveden's fame rests perhaps less on its magnificence than on its connection with the Profumo affair, one of the most infamous political scandals of the 20th century. Cliveden, as the home of Nancy Astor, the first woman to take her seat as an MP, became a centre of political and literary society, and this continued after the Second World War.

A water creature we would rather not meet!

5. Turn right, again signed 'Green Way West'. When the track bends right, turn left across a field with the usual 'Green Way West' sign.

6. At a path junction turn right over a stream, still following the 'Green Way West' signs, and follow the path ahead to a second footbridge. Immediately after crossing the bridge turn left to walk along the left-hand side of two fields to a track, passing a pond.

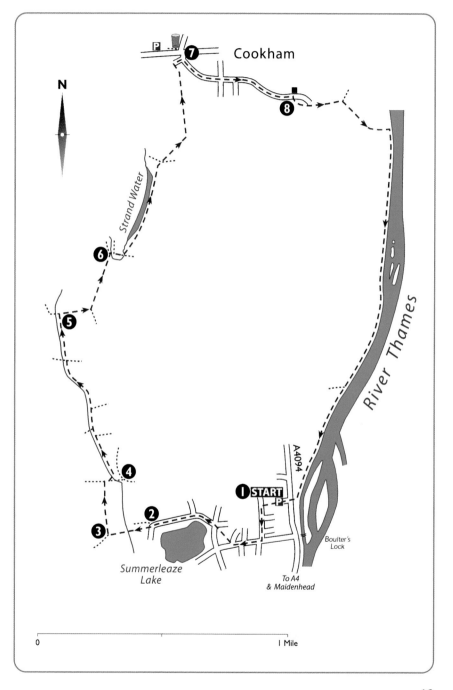

N

Cookham

7

8

Strand Water

6

5

4

3

2

Summerleaze Lake

1 **START**
P

A4094

River Thames

Boulter's Lock

To A4 & Maidenhead

0   1 Mile

It seems unbelievable today but a waterway known as The Canal ran from Cookham through central Maidenhead to the Thames at Bray. This pond, called Strand Water, was part of it. The waterway was not filled with deep water along its entire length in the way that we think of canals today. Instead, it consisted of a series of ponds that could be refilled with water from the Thames. When a boat needed to pass through, the flash lock was opened and the boat could ride the water downstream. Most of the pools have now been filled in but this one remains, albeit rather overgrown in the summer. Boats could travel upstream by being manhandled through the locks.

Cross the track and keep ahead to reach a drive to Moor Hall. Turn right to Cookham war memorial.

To explore Cookham turn right along the High Street (see walk 2, page 18). The Crown is across the road from the war memorial.

7. To continue the route, turn sharp right along a lane. Cross a main road and continue ahead along Mill Lane.

8. Opposite a house called 'The Sol Mill' turn right on the waymarked Thames Path. At a T-junction turn right to the river. Turn right by the river, back to Boulters Lock, passing the cliffs of Cliveden on the opposite side of the river.

Boulters Lock used to be called Ray Mill Lock, after the adjacent mill owned by the Ray family, who produced flour. Early records show that there was a flash lock here in the 17th century, replaced by a wooden pound lock in 1770. During Victorian times, Boulters Lock became a real honeypot as thousands of people flocked here to mess about on the river and simply see and be seen. The last salmon ladder to be built on the Thames was opened at Boulters Weir on 19th May 2000, and all the weirs from Teddington to Mapledurham now have ladders installed.

HEDSOR AND COOKHAM REACH

This varied walk has all the elements that make walking in the Chilterns so enjoyable. It includes paths through the woods, which are the glory of the Chilterns, and some fine views as well as a mile beside one of the liveliest sections of the River Thames. The route skirts the riverside communities of Bourne End and Cookham, with little town road walking, but it is easy to divert to visit either. Cookham is particularly attractive and was the home of the famous artist, Stanley Spencer.

- **DISTANCE:** 5 miles
- **MAP:** OS Explorer 172 Chiltern Hills East
- **STARTING POINT:** Furlong Road car park, Bourne End: GR 897873
- **HOW TO GET THERE:** From the eastern end of The Parade, the main road through Bourne End, at the clock take Cores End Road, signed 'High Wycombe 6', for ¼ mile. Turn right on Furlong Road to a car park immediately on the right.
- **REFRESHMENTS:** The Ferry (tel. 01628 525123) at Cookham Bridge is ideally placed about two thirds of the way round the route. The old part of the Ferry dates back to the 14th century, and the whole pub has recently been sympathetically renovated. It has a very pleasant decked area overlooking the river and the menu takes a modern approach to pub food.

THE WALK

1. Turn left out of the car park to a T-junction. Cross the road and turn left. After 20 yards, turn right on an unsigned path, passing between metal posts. Ignore all paths to left and right and continue for nearly a mile until the way ahead is barred by a gate.

This is the bed of the old Bourne End–High Wycombe railway, which opened in 1854. For 50 years it was the main train route to London for passengers from the High Wycombe area. Another, more convenient, line via Beaconsfield was opened in 1906 and the story thereafter is one of steady decline. The line closed in 1970, leaving us with this pleasant walking route.

2. Turn right to a road. Turn right and go along the road as far as a bridge across the River Wye.

The River Wye joins the Thames at Bourne End, bourn *being a dialect word for stream. For at least a thousand years the River Wye, despite its modest size, powered water mills which ground corn, fulled fabric, or, in more recent centuries, made paper. The last remaining paper mill, Glory Mill, closed in 2001.*

3. Immediately after the bridge turn left into Wooburn Park. Walk up the right-hand side of the park to find two adjacent stiles in the top right-hand corner. Do not go over either, but now bear half left across a field towards a wood, signed 'Berghers Hill ¼ mile'. Cross a stile into the wood and press on in the same direction.

4. Near the top of the hill, at a bench, turn right on a signed path. Ignore a path on the left at a second bench. When the path forks after a

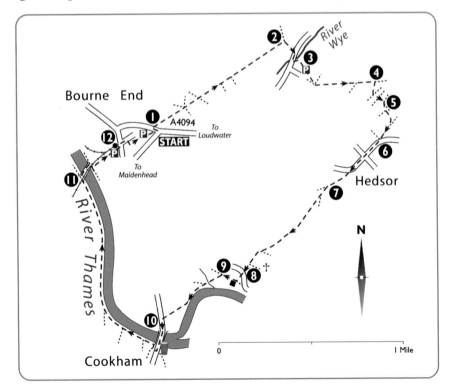

The Thames near Cookham Bridge

further 10 yards, bear round to the left to reach a gate onto a cross-track.

5. Turn right along the track. Follow it round to the right at a path junction, to reach a picnic site and a gate onto a road.

6. Go onto the road and turn right. Continue ahead at a crossroads. When the road bends right, continue ahead on Branch Lane for 200 yards.

7. Bear left on a signed path through a metal field-gate. When the path forks bear right, signed 'Church Path'. Follow this path downhill to eventually join a drive. Turn right along the drive to a road.

8. Cross the road and continue ahead, still on a drive and soon passing through some imposing gates. Follow the drive round to the right in front of a large house.

9. Shortly after the end of a brick wall on the left, turn left on a signed path. Some 10 yards after a footbridge fork left, following the waymarks for the Beeches Way and Shakespeare's Way and soon enjoying a short stretch by the River Thames. Then bear right across a field to a road.

17

Between Cookham and Cliveden the River Thames splits into four separate channels, this one being called Hedsor Water. It was the original navigation channel, and Hedsor Wharf was extremely important for trade for 500 years. However, there were many complaints about the difficulties for commercial traffic passing through Hedsor Water, which was shallow and fast flowing. The response was to create a parallel lock, cut in 1830, so that river traffic bypassed Hedsor Wharf. The then owner was aggrieved at the loss of the considerable income he had received and after a lengthy court battle he was awarded compensation.

10. Turn left over Cookham Bridge. (To visit the pretty village of Cookham continue ahead and then retrace your steps. Cookham is also visited on walk 1, page 10.) Some 40 yards after the bridge, opposite the Ferry, turn right down some steps on a signed path. At the bottom of the steps turn right to the river and then walk beside the water for a mile to the next bridge.

Cookham's most famous son was the artist Stanley Spencer, who was born in a Victorian semi on the High Street. He lived in the village for most of his life, and many of his paintings are inspired by the vistas of the church, the High Street, and the River Thames. His grave can be seen in the churchyard. The village has its own art gallery (tel. 01628 471885) dedicated to his memory. It is housed in the former Victorian Methodist chapel where Spencer was taken as a child to worship and contains a permanent collection of his work, including the famous painting entitled Christ Preaching at Cookham Regatta, *together with letters, documents, memorabilia, and the pram in which Spencer wheeled his equipment when painting landscapes. It is open daily in summer and at weekends in winter.*

11. Recross the river beside the railway. Over the bridge turn right for 20 yards; then turn left up some steps. Follow the path to Bourne End station car park and walk across the car park to a road.

12. Turn left for 15 yards, then turn right along Boston Drive and continue for 80 yards. Now turn right on a signed path. Follow this as it turns left to emerge on the road by the car park where this walk started.

LITTLE MARLOW

The Thames has deposited gravel beds along its valley and these are dug out for use as a building material. A gravel extraction pit is not a pretty sight when the diggers are at work, but with careful management it is possible to turn a disused quarry into a place of tranquil beauty, a haven for wildlife and fishermen. This level walk explores some of the lakes created between Marlow and Bourne End and visits the pretty village of Little Marlow. It returns beside the Thames, along the reach overlooked by the thickly wooded slopes of Winter Hill on the opposite bank.

- **DISTANCE:** 4 miles
- **MAP:** OS Explorer 172 Chiltern Hills East
- **STARTING POINT:** Spade Oak car park, Coldmoorholme Lane, Bourne End. This is not the pub car park but a public one, a short distance beyond on the other side of the road: GR 883875
- **HOW TO GET THERE:** From the A4155, Marlow–Bourne End road, about ¾ mile west of Bourne End, turn south along Coldmoorholme Lane to the car park on the right after about ½ mile.
- **REFRESHMENTS:** This walk passes two pubs: the Spade Oak (tel. 01628 520090) at the start, and the Queen's Head (tel. 01628 482927) in Little Marlow. Both have gardens and serve food. The Queen's Head is particularly charming, with roses round the door and an enterprising lunch menu.

THE WALK

1. Return to the lane and turn left to walk back along the lane past the Spade Oak pub. Opposite the thatched lychgate to The Old Thatch, turn left on a signed path to a metal kissing-gate. Go through the gate and walk across a field to another kissing gate onto a cross-path.

The Spade Oak was once known as the Ferry Hotel, advertised in Kelly's Directory of 1895 as 'a riverside hotel for boating, fishing and launch parties'. After the First World War a former gaiety girl of the Edwardian stage, Muriel Maud Joycey, bought it. She renamed it the Spade Oak, converting it into a wonderful country hotel, with a ballroom, swimming pool, and children's boating pond complete with paddleboats. Next to the pub, the Old Thatch was the home of children's author Enid Blyton between 1929 and 1938. It is now owned by a garden designer and the gardens are open to the public on summer weekends.

2. Turn right and follow the path round Spade Oak Lake to a fork.

Gravel extraction, which began here in 1966, has left this lake as a legacy. Little Marlow Parish Council, working with the owners, Lafarge Aggregates, developed the path around the lake as their millennium project. It attracts a very wide range of birds, from the large mute swan to the tiny goldcrest.

3. Bear right, away from the lake, to shortly reach a footbridge and a T-junction with a cross-path. Turn left. Continue across the access road to the Lafarge site and more footbridges to reach a lane.

Spade Oak Lake

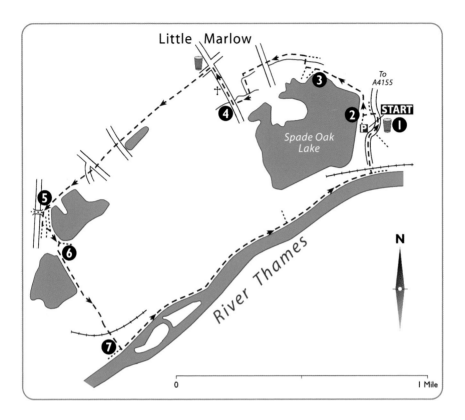

4. Turn right into Little Marlow. Turn left along Pound Lane. At the Queen's Head carry on along a track and keep in the same direction across a lane and access drives to eventually reach a footbridge over the Marlow bypass after about a mile.

The bustling riverside town up the river is technically Great Marlow and this is its smaller and more tranquil neighbour, a pretty village with a 17th-century manor house, village green, and 12th-century church. The church is usually locked but have a look at the unusual lychgate.

5. Do not cross the footbridge but turn left and go ahead for 75 yards. Now bear left, away from the bypass, on, at the time of writing, quite a faint path and follow this across four paths in very close proximity to each other, to join a lakeside path. Turn right along it, with the lake on your left, to shortly reach a footbridge.

21

The Thames seen at point 7 of the walk

6. Some 15 yards after crossing a footbridge turn right and follow this narrow but clear path to the railway, passing another lake on the right. Cross the line and go ahead to a gate onto a playing field. Through the gate turn left along the left-hand side of the field to the riverside path.

7. Turn left and walk by the river for 1¼ miles, as far as the first lane. Turn left, over the railway, to go back to the car park where this walk started.

This is Coldmoorholme Lane. There has been much debate about whether the name should be with or without the final e, to the extent that some 20 years ago each of the two nameplates at the top of the lane spelled it differently. The original name for the area was Cold Moorholm; so where the 'e' came from is uncertain. At the end of the lane there used to be an important wharf receiving goods from London and exporting timber and produce from the surrounding countryside, as well as the Spade Oak ferry. The ferry closed in 1956, and so we can no longer cross the river here.

THE THAMES AT MEDMENHAM

This gentle stroll explores one of the most tranquil and beautiful stretches of the Chiltern Thames, as well as the village of Medmenham, which has many attractive houses. The river, shaded by mature trees, makes a fine landscape, with the Chiltern hills rising beyond. The return uses easy field paths. Short and almost completely level, this makes an ideal expedition to dawdle away a summer afternoon, perhaps with a picnic to enjoy by the river, or maybe an evening stroll rounded off with a pub meal.

- **DISTANCE:** 3 miles
- **MAPS:** OS Explorer 171 Chiltern Hills West and 172 Chiltern Hills East.
- **STARTING POINT:** Medmenham church: GR 804844
- **HOW TO GET THERE:** From the A4155 Marlow–Henley road, turn south at the church in Medmenham along the lane through the village. There are several spots along the lane where it is possible to park without causing inconvenience.
- **REFRESHMENTS:** There are no refreshments directly on the route, but the village pub, the Dog and Badger (tel. 01491 571362), is a few steps away on the main road. The pub dates from the 14th century and the present building is mainly 17th-century.

THE WALK

People have lived here by the Thames from time immemorial. Up on the hill overlooking the village to the west of Bockmer Lane are the remains of an Iron Age hill fort. The church is supposed to have been founded in AD 640 by Saint Birinus, and the present structure dates from the 12th century with, of course, many later additions. There is provision for four bells but for many centuries there have been only three in place. Tradition says that the fourth bell was sold to raise funds to help pay the ransom to free Richard the Lionheart when he was taken prisoner on his return from the crusades.

1. Walk through the village to the end of the lane and the River Thames.

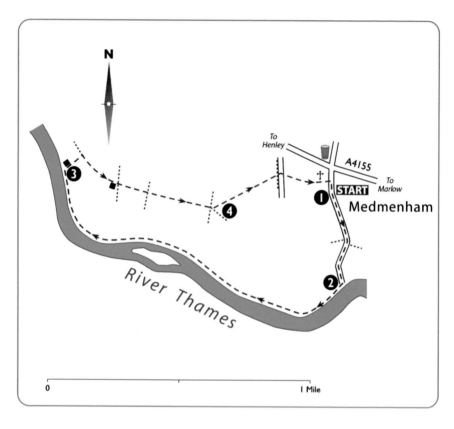

On the left as you approach the river is the site of the infamous *Medmenham Abbey. Its notoriety does not come from the Cistercian monks who founded it in the 13th century, but from the activities of the so-called Hell Fire Club. Sir Francis Dashwood succeeded to his father's estate and fortune when he was sixteen. His considerable energy, wealth, and achievement (he became Chancellor of the Exchequer) were matched by his profligacy. Dashwood's home was at West Wycombe, but in the 1750s he leased the site of the abbey and proceeded to turn it into a venue for the Brotherhood of St Francis or Dashwood's Apostles.*

The members, or 'monks', were among the most prominent men in the country. Half of Dashwood's Cabinet colleagues were members, as was Benjamin Franklin, who was the London agent for a number of American colonies. This was the ideal, discreet site, since it could be approached from the river and was screened by trees.

A tranquil scene near Medmenham

Workmen were sent in; the abbey site was rebuilt and the grounds landscaped to make it suitable for the wild parties held there. Apparently, marble pillars were erected on which were carved pornographic inscriptions in bastard, or 'macaroni', Latin and small temples were put up here and there. The groves were filled with statuary in indecent poses. There was a Roman room, whose walls were hung with paintings copied from ancient and indecent Roman frescoes and paintings of famous English prostitutes. The abbey's library supposedly contained one of the most complete collections of pornography in England.

For his monks there had to be plenty of 'nuns'. Most were prostitutes and others were the wives, sisters, and fiancées of members who wanted to join in the fun. Later the group fell apart with accusations of Satanism. They were undoubtedly up to no good but wild parties are more likely than devil worship, which was probably a political slur rather than a statement of fact (see walk 15, page 71).

2. Turn right and go along the riverside path for about 1¼ miles.

This was the site of one of the ferries that carried passengers across the river. The monument here was erected by the first Viscount Devonport in 1899 to commemorate his success in proving in court that the Medmenham ferry was a public amenity and so he no longer had to fund its upkeep.

3. In front of a thatched house follow the path round to the right, away from the river, for 200 yards. Level with a metal kissing-gate onto a track, turn right across a field, heading just to the left of a small brick building. Cross a concrete track and continue in the same direction to cross a second track and reach a third.

4. At the far side of the track the path forks: bear left across a field to a permitted cross-path and drive. Continue in the same direction on a signed path to reach the lane through Medmenham and return to the start.

HAMBLEDEN AND ASTON

The water courses explored on this figure of eight walk could not be in greater contrast. The longer southern loop is by the mighty Thames, the southern boundary of the Chilterns, while the shorter northern loop is partly beside Hamble Brook, a winterbourne that does not necessarily flow in dry years. As well as being a waterside walk, it is also partly an across-water walk, as it uses the long bridge over the weir, a distance of perhaps 200 yards, to connect the two loops. It is, of course, perfectly possible to do the two loops separately if you wish, using the car park at Mill End near points 4 and 10. A particularly pleasing feature of this walk are the good views of typical Chilterns scenery of hills, fields, and woods, seen from several points. The route also visits three villages, two of which have good pubs.

- **DISTANCE:** 6 miles
- **MAP:** OS Explorer 171 Chiltern Hills West
- **STARTING POINT:** Hambleden village car park next to the Stag and Huntsman pub: GR 785865
- **HOW TO GET THERE:** At Mill End, 3 miles from Henley or 5 miles from Marlow on the A4155 Henley–Marlow road, turn up the road signed 'Hambleden 1, Skirmett 3, Fingest 3'. Turn right into Hambleden village on a road signed 'Pheasant's Hill 1, Frieth 3, Lane End 4'. In the centre of the village, when the main road bends left, continue ahead past the Stag and Huntsman to a car park on the right.
- **REFRESHMENTS:** The Stag and Huntsman (tel. 01491 571227) is in Hambleden, at the start of the walk, and the Flowerpot (tel. 01491 574721) is in Aston, about three-quarters of the way round. Both have pleasant gardens and serve food. In addition, the shop in Hambleden serves teas, with tables outside overlooking the centre of the pretty village.

THE WALK

1. Return to the entrance to the car park and turn right along the lane for 100 yards. Turn right on a signed path along a track.

2. At a T-junction turn left uphill. When the track ends after about 100

yards, turn right on a signed path along the right-hand side of a field and go through a metal kissing-gate into a wood. Some 15 yards into the wood, turn right on a waymarked path, through another kissing gate out of the wood. Beyond the gate turn left to walk along the left-hand side of two fields, with excellent views to the right, to a lane.

Hambleden Mill

3. Turn right. At the main road turn left.

4. At the A4155 turn right, and, in a few yards, turn left on a signed path between houses. Follow this as it bears right between a fence and a wall to the bridge over the weir and across to the lock.

In the past the Thames did not look like it does today. It meandered along through many channels with marshes on either side and was shallow in the summer and often flooded in winter. Despite this, before proper roads were built, it was an important route for people and goods to move around the country. Not only that, the flowing water was a vital source of power and so millers built weirs to try to maintain a steady flow. This, of course, was a source of conflict between those wishing to exploit the water for power and those who wanted to use it as a highway. To try to meet both needs flash locks were used: impounded water was released in a flash that the boat could ride downstream. The locks were difficult and dangerous to use and still interfered with the activities of other river users, which was the cause of many disputes. Modern pound locks were introduced from the 17th century onwards, though the last flash lock on the Thames was not replaced until the 20th century.

5. Cross the lock. Turn right and walk upstream beside the Thames to Remenham.

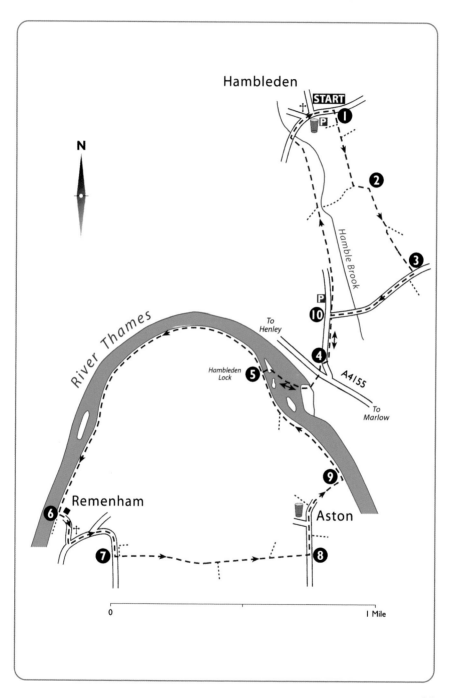

The white 'temple' on the island in the river was built in 1771 as a vista and fishing lodge for Fawley Court and is the start of the Henley regatta course (see walk 6, page 35). Today the island is owned by the Henley Regatta, and is rented out for corporate entertaining.

6. Immediately after the second house, turn left on a signed path along a track leading to a lane. Continue in the same direction through the village, passing the church on the left. At a T-junction turn left; then in 100 yards turn right onto Remenham Church Lane and follow this uphill and through a small wood.

There has been a community here for a long time, as there is evidence of a Roman settlement and the name may be derived from the Remi, the Celtic people who once lived here. The village is mentioned in the Domesday Book (1086) and the charters of Westminster Abbey dated 1075. The church has a recorded history of more than 1,000 years and rests on Saxon and Norman foundations, though the building we see today is 19th-century. The entire population was wiped out in an outbreak of plague in the 17th century and the village never recovered from this disaster; so Remenham today is a few cottages clustering round the church.

7. Some 60 yards after leaving the wood, turn left over a stile by a gate on a signed path. Follow the track ahead. When the track bends right, continue ahead on a path. Ignore a permitted path to the left and press on ahead through a gate and down the left-hand side of two fields to a lane.

8. Turn left and walk through Aston. Continue ahead to the right of the Flowerpot and follow Ferry Lane to the river.

9. Turn left to Hambleden Lock. Recross the lock and retrace your steps to the junction of the lane, Rotten Row, and the road mentioned at point 3.

Hambleden Lock with its white weather-boarded mill reflected in the river is a most attractive and much photographed view from the bridge. The mill originally dates from 1388. The present structure is 16th-century and was working until 1958. The building is now converted into flats.

Hamble Brook

10. At this junction take a signed path through a field gate on the right and, crossing a track, continue in the same direction over the fields to Hambleden, seen ahead. At the lane in Hambleden turn right through the village to go back to the car park.

This path eventually converges with Hamble Brook, usually flowing on the far side of the field to begin with. Hamble Brook is a winterbourne, though, that only flows when the water table is high enough; so it may not be flowing at all!

Hambleden means the village in the valley and that describes its situation perfectly, with the old cottages clustered round the square and church and the green hills rising behind. There has probably been a church here since Saxon times and the present structure is basically Norman with, of course, many later additions. It is sometimes referred to as the Cathedral of the Chilterns and is well worth visiting for several interesting features, including what is supposed to be part of Cardinal Wolsey's bed head. Notice the pump in the square. Even though Hambleden stands on a stream, the villagers could not rely on it for water and needed the pump as well.

HENLEY AND FAWLEY

If you love trees as well as walking by water, this is the walk for you. It starts on the outskirts of Henley-on-Thames and climbs through woods and across fields to Fawley, high on the Chiltern Hills overlooking the Thames. The route then descends through beautiful beech woods to Greenlands and crosses the parkland with many magnificent specimen trees before returning to Henley along the world-famous regatta course.

This is a lovely walk at any time of year except the first week in July during Henley Regatta, when the town is full to bursting and the banks of the river are taken over by the associated social events.

- **DISTANCE:** 7 miles
- **MAP:** OS Explorer 171 Chiltern Hills West
- **STARTING POINT:** Dry Leas car park, Henley: GR 760832
- **HOW TO GET THERE:** Dry Leas car park (charge) is at the edge of Henley on the A4155 to Marlow, 100 yards from its junction with the A4120. It is next to Henley Rugby Club.
- **REFRESHMENTS:** There are numerous pubs and cafés of all sorts in Henley, and, just after the start, the route passes the Old White Horse (tel. 01491 575763), which serves food and has a garden.

THE WALK

1. Return to the road and turn right. At a roundabout turn right again by the A4120.

This broad road is aptly named Fair Mile. It is supposed to be the route of the Roman road from Dorchester that crossed the Thames at Henley. Beside Fair Mile is the course of Assendon Stream, which is another of the Chilterns' occasional 'rivers'. It flows down from Stonor when the water table is high enough and rarely reaches its natural outlet into the Thames before sinking into the chalk. It flows only about once in 40 years but when it does it can cause flooding in the Assendons and on Fairmile This is largely because in the intervening years the open ditches and enclosed culverts through which it should flow have fallen into disrepair and ceased to be of real use.

Round House Farm at point 6 of the walk

2. Opposite Fair Mile Court turn right onto the Oxfordshire Way. Do not go into a field but keep to the right on a fenced path and continue on this path uphill when the fence on the right ends. Follow the path through a wood to a kissing gate; then walk on in the same direction to eventually join a surfaced drive. Keep going in the same direction past Henley Park, and then ahead when the drive becomes a track.

3. About ½ mile after passing Henley Park, turn right over a stile and go ahead to the right of a hedge to a second stile. Over this stile, keep ahead to a track. Cross the track and now, crossing two stiles, walk down the right-hand side of a field into a dip and up the other side to a sunken lane. Cross the lane and continue in the same direction to emerge on a drive at a junction.

4. Turn left and walk up to a lane.

5. Turn right. Continue for a mile along the lane through Fawley, passing the church on the left and ignoring a lane to the left and one to the right.

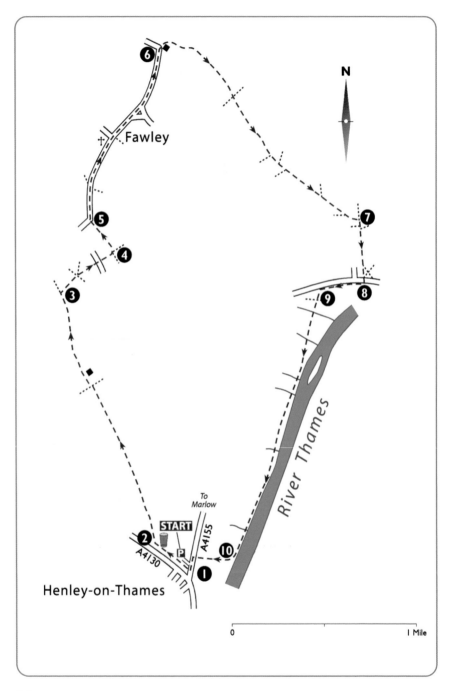

N

Fawley

River Thames

To Marlow

START

A4155

A4130

P

Henley-on-Thames

0   I Mile

Fawley is a scattered hilltop village, probably of Saxon origin. Villages on top of the dry Chiltern Hills often had a problem with water. Next to the church is a pond, which may be choked with vegetation. Most hilltop ponds such as this are man-made to water cattle. Note the well under a pretty pagoda on the village green on the right: it is said to be 338 ft deep. There has been a church on this site for 800 years. The earliest parts of the present building date from the late 12th or early 13th centuries. The most unusual features of Fawley church are the mausoleums in the churchyard, both built by families who once owned the estate.

6. When the lane bends left at Round House Farm, bear right on a signed bridleway. When the track ends continue ahead on a path and follow this down through beech woods, ignoring tracks and paths to left and right. Carry on downhill out of the woods, joining a track coming in from the right, to a T-junction with a cross-track.

7. Turn right. When the track bends left, go ahead to the main road.

This is part of the Greenlands estate. It was once owned by W.H. Smith, the stationer and MP, who was satirized by Gilbert and Sullivan in HMS Pinafore *because 'he never went to sea and rose to be Ruler of the Queen's Navee'. He is buried in the churchyard at Hambleden (see walk 5, page 31). Note the intertwined initials over the door of the cottage on the right of the track. The house, on the far side of the main road, is now Henley Management College.*

8. Cross the road and turn right; continue along the footway for ¼ mile to a path starting over a stile on the left.

9. Over the stile bear half right. Cross a drive and keep on in the same direction, crossing three footbridges, to reach the Thames at Temple Island (see walk 5, page 30). Press on along the path, now by the river.

The stately home passed on the right is Fawley Court, formerly the home of the Freeman family, whose mausoleum was passed earlier in the walk. The house is now a Catholic college. This stretch of river is the famous Henley regatta course. Henley Royal Regatta is a great rowing festival, and social occasion, which had its origin in the first University Boat Race, in June 1829. After that race the people of Henley realized

Temple Island

that they had one of the finest stretches of river for racing in the world. In 1839 a public meeting was held in the town hall, attended by the local landed gentry and prominent townspeople. It was decided to establish a regatta with the aims of 'producing most beneficial effects to the town' and being 'a source of amusement and gratification to the neighbourhood'. The first regatta took place on 14th June 1839, with four races held between 4 pm and 7 pm. It has now grown to five days of racing held in the first week of July, with more than 350 entries from all over the world. The 'royal' part of its title originated in 1861 when Prince Albert became its patron.

10. When the way ahead is barred, turn right to the main road. Turn left back to the entrance to the car park.

GORING

This walk starts along one of the most beautiful stretches of the River Thames – the incomparable Goring Gap, where the river breaks through the chalk to separate the Chilterns from the Berkshire Downs. The views from this path are lovely and encompass both the river and the Chilterns above. This area of typical woods and fields is explored on the return leg. This walk is the longest in the book but I cannot recommend it too highly. There are a few climbs but nothing too strenuous.

- **DISTANCE:** 7½ miles
- **MAP:** OS Explorer 171 Chiltern Hills West
- **STARTING POINT:** Goring village car park (charge):GR 599807
- **HOW TO GET THERE:** From the main road through Goring, the B4009, opposite the Miller of Mansfield pub, turn along Manor Road. Take the first on the left to the car park entrance on the left, next to the Catherine Wheel pub.
- **REFRESHMENTS:** There are several pubs in Goring that serve food, notably the historic Miller of Mansfield (tel. 01491 872829) and the Catherine Wheel (tel. 01491 872379). The village bakery (tel. 01491 874264) in the small modern shopping arcade also serves teas and excellent baguettes and pastries. There is no refreshment on the rest of the walk.

THE WALK

1. With your back to the entrance to the car park, take a path to the right of the public conveniences to the main road through Goring. Turn left. Before the bridge over the Thames, bear left on a minor road to the river.

This has been a major crossing point of the Thames since time immemorial and the Romans built a causeway across the river. Goring used to be linked to its twin, Streatley, by a ferry and this was the scene of a great disaster in 1674 when the boat capsized and all 60 people on board were drowned. The ferry was replaced by a toll bridge in 1837.

2. Turn left along the riverbank. After about a mile the path goes under a railway bridge.

Known locally as the Four Arches, this railway bridge is built on the skew and is a good example of Victorian craftsmanship. In fact, there are two bridges, built with different brick patterns, as the bridge was widened when the track was increased. You will also note several pillboxes from the

Goring Lock

Second World War by the river. As part of the plans for responding to an invasion, the Thames was designated the line to which the defensive forces would retreat if the Channel coast was lost, and plans were made to blow up every bridge over the river.

3. In another ¼ mile, at Ferry Cottage, the path is forced to the left, away from the riverbank, to a T-junction after about 100 yards. Turn right. The path eventually comes back to the river but some distance above it in woodland. Continue along the path as it veers away from the river and then drops into a dip and climbs steeply up some steps on the other side.

This is Hartslock Wood. In the early 1500s the Hart family owned a lock across the river near here. In 1710 it was reported to be a fishing lock – a wooden construction used to support nets and eel traps. By 1802 the ruins of this lock were known as Hart's Old Weir. The ruins were an inconvenience to traffic on the river and accordingly, in 1804 and again in 1812, orders were given for the timbers to be removed. Obviously this work was not successfully carried out because in 1910 a Mr Thacker watched its final destruction. Barges were moored in the river 'drawing the teeth of this half-extinct monster against the left bank'.

4. At the top, the path joins the track to Hartslock Farm. Go ahead along the track in the same direction for ¾ mile to a road.

5. Turn left and go up the road for ¼ mile. There is a good path on the right-hand side of the road.

6. Some 100 yards after the roadside path ends, just beyond the entrance to Stoneycroft, bear left uphill on a path signed 'Cold Harbour 1¼'. Bear left to a small metal gate and continue along the left-hand side of a field. At the far end continue along a fenced path to a farm. Cross a farm drive and press on ahead on a signed path towards and through a wood, ignoring paths on the right.

7. Cross a stile out of the wood. The path is not visible on the ground but heads across two fields toward the right-hand side of some farm

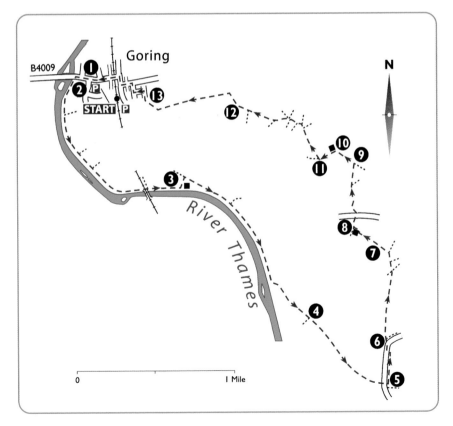

buildings. Do not go through the gate but take a stile on the right and turn left to walk round the left-hand side of a field to a stile by a gate onto a farm track.

8. Turn right along the track. Cross a lane and continue on the farm drive on the other side to a T-junction with a surfaced drive.

9. Turn left.

10. The drive ends at a farm. Some 50 yards before the farm, go through a wooden gate on the left and walk over to a gate that gives onto a sunken path. Follow this downhill.

11. About 20 yards after a gate across the path, turn right on a clear path marked by blue waymarks on a post. Bear left at a fork in the path marked by yellow waymarks on a post. Cross a track and bear left at a fork after a further 20 yards. Bear right at the next fork. Stay on the path marked by Chiltern Way marks, ignoring all side turns and cross-paths, for ½ mile to a gate out of the wood.

12. Follow the path up the right-hand side of a field and then turn left along the top of the field. At the far end continue along the right-hand side of a second field. There are wonderful views from this point and Goring can be seen below. Go through a hedge gap onto a playing field. Go across or round – depending on the state of play – to a gate on the far side.

The hillside you can see to your left is Hartslock Nature Reserve, famous for its orchids. The south facing chalk slopes are a wonderful place for wild flowers. Sadly, much of this habitat has been lost under the plough, but look closely at the field edges in the summer and you will see that they contain a profusion of wild flowers such as scabious, milkwort and speedwell.

13. At the end of a short, hedged path, join a road on an estate of large, modern houses. Follow the road round to the left and turn right at a T-junction. At the main road turn left. Turn right at the Queens Arms and then left over the railway. Follow this road down into Goring.

CHALFONT PARK AND THE COLNE VALLEY

Starting in the dormitory town of Gerrards Cross, this route is immensely varied. Soon leaving the leafy suburbs behind, the route crosses the River Misbourne, here dammed to make a lake, before climbing through typical Chilterns scenery and then dropping down again to the valley of the River Colne. The towpath of the Grand Union Canal is a chance to stride out with the canal on one side and lakes on the other (omitted from the map for clarity). A delightful woodland path leads to Denham station, and a train ride back to Gerrards Cross completes an interesting expedition. Telephone: National Rail Enquiries on 08457 484950 for times of trains.

- **DISTANCE:** 7 miles
- **STARTING POINT:** Gerrards Cross station. Gerrards Cross is on the High Wycombe line from Marylebone. There is a car park adjacent (charge): GR 002888.
- **HOW TO GET THERE:** From the traffic lights on the A40 at Gerrards Cross, turn north along the B416 (Packhorse Road) to the station and the car park beyond it, down a road on the left.
- **MAP:** OS Explorer 172 Chiltern Hills East
- **REFRESHMENTS:** There are numerous possibilities in Gerrards Cross at the start of the walk. Part way round the walk the route passes the Coy Carp pub (tel. 01895 821471), enviably positioned with gardens between the canal and river and serving food all day. Further on, the towpath passes the Horse and Barge pub as well.

THE WALK

1. Walk up the station approach to the main road and turn left.

2. Some 30 yards after South Park Crescent, opposite Orchehill Avenue, turn right on a fenced, signed path. Continue ahead across a road to another road. Turn right and in 15 yards turn left to continue in the same direction, bearing right at a fork after 10 yards to reach a dual carriageway.

3. Cross the road to a footpath on the other side and follow this over a stile, across a small field, over a drive, and half right across a second field to a stile onto a track.

The house that can be seen to the left along the drive is Chalfont Park, once owned by a member of the Churchill family. The old part of the building dates from 1755 and the lake, fed by the River Misbourne, was constructed about the same time. The house was redesigned by John Nash in the 1800s, in the then fashionable 'Strawberry Hill' Gothic style. It has been used as a military hospital and a hotel and is now the centrepiece of an office complex.

4. Turn left, passing the end of a lake. Continue ahead uphill when the track turns right towards Meadow Grange. Ignore all paths to the left; then follow the path as it bends left to eventually emerge at a drive in front of a modern building, which is a nursing home.

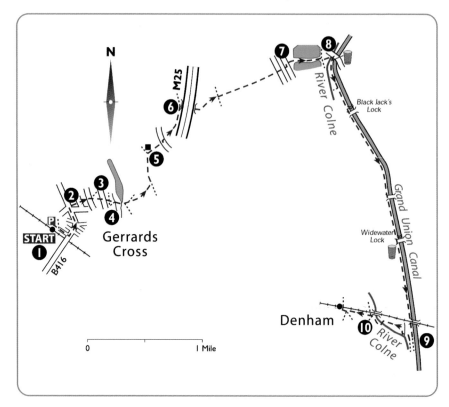

5. Turn right along the drive to a road. Cross the road to a path 10 yards to the left to continue in the same direction for about ¼ mile to a path junction.

6. Turn right, walking through a subway under the M25. Continue ahead, signed 'Pynesfield Lake' at a cross-path, to a road. Cross the road and keep ahead to a lane.

This is the valley of the River Colne, which rises at London Colney in Hertfordshire and enters the Thames at Staines. The extraction of gravel has had an enormous influence on the landscape. The flooding of former gravel pits has resulted in a string of over 50 lakes, many of which are important for wildlife and are very attractive. This lake is the first of several passed on the route.

7. Turn left and in 25 yards turn right, signed 'Coppermill Lane', soon to walk on an embankment between lakes. When this path ends at a surfaced track, turn right and in 20 yards turn left. Cross a drive and press on past the pub to a road.

The River Colne and the Grand Union Canal are very close together here, with water flowing into and out of the canal to provide a supply of water and regulate flows. Note the slalom poles over the canal at a water

Pynesfield Lake

outlet where canoeists practise their white-water manoeuvring. After the arrival of the canal improved the transport links, a mill on the Colne was converted to produce copper, hence the name. The metal was used to cover the bottom of Royal Navy ships and for the dome of St Paul's Cathedral in London.

Black Jack's Lock on the Grand Union Canal

8. Turn right over a bridge across a river. Before a second bridge, over the canal, turn right along a towpath and follow this for about 2½ miles.

The canal, then known as the Grand Junction Canal, reached here at the end of the 18th century. It was built by teams of men called navigators, or 'navvies', using picks, shovels, and an enormous amount of muscle power. The route through to Birmingham was completed in 1803 and was a vital transport link between London and the Midlands until superseded by the railway and improved roads.

9. Some 300 yards after passing beneath a magnificent grey-brick railway viaduct, turn right on a clear path starting down eight shallow steps. After 70 yards turn right at a T-junction and follow the path as it wends, apparently aimlessly, through the woods and over two bridges to arrive in front of another grey-brick viaduct.

10. Turn left and follow the path to a T-junction with a surfaced path. Turn right to Denham station and catch the train back to Gerrards Cross.

This railway line was opened in 1906. Denham Parish Council were consulted about the railway and they asked that the arch be high enough to take a fully laden hay wagon. The coming of the railway transformed Gerrards Cross from a crossroads on the London–Oxford road to a highly desirable place to live in beautiful countryside within very easy reach of London.

BERKHAMSTED

This easy walk is exceptionally varied and interesting. It starts along a quiet, ancient lane which is little more than a surfaced path. It then wends its way through woodlands and across a golf course before making its way into Berkhamsted by its ancient Norman castle. It ends with a relaxed stroll along the towpath of one of England's great canals, the Grand Union.

- **DISTANCE:** 5 miles
- **MAPS:** OS Explorer 181 Chiltern Hills North and 182 St Albans and Hatfield
- **STARTING POINT:** The parking area at the junction of Bullbeggars Lane and Bank Mill Lane, Berkhamsted: GR0069071.
- **HOW TO GET THERE:** From the A4251 at the extreme eastern end of Berkhamsted, turn north on a minor road called Bullbeggars Lane. Very soon cross a small bridge over a stream and immediately park on the left in a wide layby at the junction of Bullbeggars Lane and Bank Mill Lane.
- **REFRESHMENTS:** There are three pubs overlooking the canal which are passed towards the end of the walk: the Crystal Palace (tel. 01442 862998), the Boat (tel. 01442 877152), and the Rising Sun (tel. 01442 864913). All serve food. There is no source of refreshment earlier in the walk.

THE WALK

1. From the parking place continue along Bullbeggars Lane, soon crossing the canal and the railway. Continue along this very quiet lane for about a mile.

2. Opposite the entrance to Roseheath Wood, a large house on the right, take a signed path on the left along the right-hand side of a field. At the end of the field continue ahead through a wood, following the clear path down into a dip. At the end of the wood continue in a narrow belt of trees, now going uphill. When the path enters woodland again, keep ahead to a track. Carry on in the same direction along the track to a lane.

3. Turn right to a road and cross the road. Do not take the signed bridleway ahead but instead take an unsigned path 10 yards to the right. Follow this as it bears right to a T-junction with a cross-path.

4. Turn right. Follow the main path for about ½ mile, ignoring all side paths that go left to a golf course and right to the road, and watch for some wires supported by telegraph poles crossing above the path. About 10 yards after passing beneath the wires, bear left at a fork. Keep on in the same direction until the path ends in front of a fence at the rear of houses.

5. Turn left here on a cross-path. This is a bridleway and can be very muddy: the first and worst section can be avoided by following the

The remains of Berkhamsted Castle

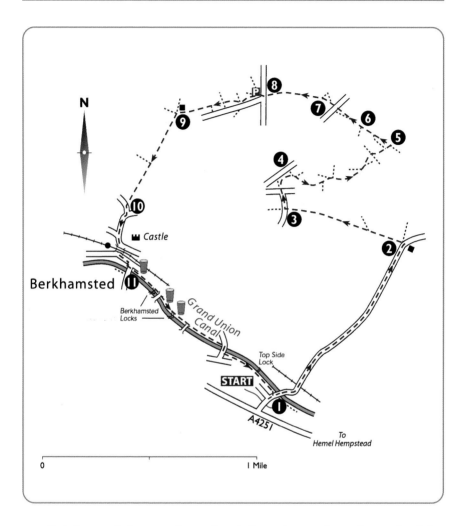

parallel footpath just to the right. Follow this path to the end of the wood.

6. Just before the end of the wood, bear left onto a sunken path and follow the path across the golf course and through more woods to a lane, again escaping mud by taking the parallel walkers' path to the right.

7. Cross the road to where two public bridleways leave the lane. Take the left-hand one and follow it across a mosaic of fairways and small areas of woodland to a war memorial and road.

47

8. Cross the road to a small car park opposite, slightly to the right. Take a path in the far left corner; after 10 yards bear left on a narrow and possibly muddy path and follow it downhill through woods, ignoring a signed bridleway on the right. Continue across a cross-path marked with blue arrows, and go out of the wood and onto a farm track. Keep ahead on the track to the bottom of a small valley.

9. At the bottom of the valley, just after some barns on the right, turn left over a stile. Walk along the right-hand side of three fields and on in the same direction between cricket pitches and along a drive to a road.

10. Turn left. At the main road continue in the same direction with the remains of the castle on your left. The entrance to the castle is a few yards along the road to the left, just before the railway line. After exploring the ruins, go under the railway and turn left by the canal.

Berkhamsted was the site of a very significant event in English history. On a cold November day in 1066 all that remained of King Harold's noblemen surrendered here to William the Conqueror, who promised to be a 'Kind Lord' to them. One of their number, Bishop Ealdred, went on to crown William at Westminster on Christmas Day.

William divided the land up between his supporters. He gave Berkhamsted to Robert of Mortrain, his half brother, who built the first castle, protected by a wooden palisade cut from the surrounding beechwoods. In the next century it was held by Thomas à Becket under Henry II and it was rebuilt with a stone keep and walls. These could not have been very well constructed because they were breached by the barons in their fight with King John and had to be rebuilt. The castle was in continuous use as a royal residence until the end of the 15th century, when it was allowed to fall into disrepair. The walls were again breached by Cromwell's guns in the Civil War, and time and the use of the stone in the town have left little of what was once such an important fortification. The main gateway and part of the southern defences were pulled down in the 19th century to make way for the railway, and the ragged walls and empty moat now surround a smooth green lawn with a pretty cottage and the mound of Shell Keep.

11. At the first bridge go down onto the towpath, noting the totem pole carved by Canadian Indians in 1967: a startling sight in an English country town! At bridge number 143, cross the canal to continue along

The towpath near point 11 of the route

the towpath in the same direction. At the next bridge, number 144, leave the towpath and go up to the road. Turn right, back to the start.

The canal is the Grand Union Canal. For more information see the introduction and the information boards by the canal.

NORTHCHURCH COMMON AND COW ROAST LOCK

This is a very varied route that includes a most enjoyable walk of about two miles along the towpath of the Grand Union Canal. It passes several locks as the canal climbs to its summit, and most of them have seats so you can rest in comfort to watch the boats navigate them, always an entertaining pastime. In addition, the route explores part of the Ashridge Estate, managed by the National Trust, with superb woods and open common land. A leafy lane connects the two elements of this interesting walk.

- **DISTANCE:** 5 miles
- **MAP:** OS Explorer 181 Chiltern Hills North
- **STARTING POINT:** Northchurch Common parking area: GR 978102
- **HOW TO GET THERE:** The parking area is on the B4506 Northchurch–Ashridge road, about a mile north of its junction with the A4251 in Northchurch. It is not easy to spot. Take a track almost opposite the entrance to Hill Farm and turn immediately right to an informal parking area.
- **REFRESHMENTS:** There are no refreshments on the route. The Cow Roast Inn (tel. 01442 822287) lies a couple of hundred yards off the route and now specializes in Thai food. It also serves sandwiches and has a garden.

THE WALK

1. Return to the road and turn right, and in 30 yards turn left onto a signed bridleway. Follow this path through the woods to a surfaced drive leading to Northchurch Farm. Cross the drive and press on along the path, which eventually becomes a track, to a T-junction with a lane to the right and a track to the left.

2. Cross the lane and carry on in the same direction on a signed bridleway to reach a fork after 60 yards. Bear left and follow the path round to the left to arrive at a road junction.

3. Cross Haynes Mead and walk downhill on a road called Bridleway. At the end of the road continue in the same direction across a small open area and along a road; go over the railway to a bridge over the canal.

4. Over the canal turn left, back on yourself, to the towpath. Turn left and continue along the towpath for about two miles, crossing from the left bank to the right bank of the canal at Dudswell Lock.

This is the valley of the River Bulbourne, an insignificant stream today. It rises near Cow Roast, where we shall leave the canal. If you wish to have a look at it, go over a stile just before Dudswell Lock, and a plank bridge crosses the river after a few yards. The Grand Union Canal took much of the river's water supply when it was constructed in 1797. In its heyday, before the canal, the River Bulbourne was a full and fast moving river yielding a healthy crop of eels and other fish.

Bushes Lock

5. At bridge 137 go under the bridge and up to a lane. Turn left for 200 yards. (To visit the Cow Roast Inn turn right on the main road.) Turn left over a stile on a signed path and walk across a field to a footbridge over the railway. Over the bridge continue across a second field to a T-junction with a cross-path. Turn right to a second T-junction. Turn right again and follow the path beside the railway to a lane.

This is Cow Roast Lock. It does not, as might be imagined, get its name from some gigantic barbecue but is a corruption of 'cow rest', having been a favourite resting place of drovers as they took cattle through the Chilterns to the London markets. This has always been an important route through the Chilterns, as we can see from the road, canal, and railway all close together. The road was the Roman Akeman Street, and

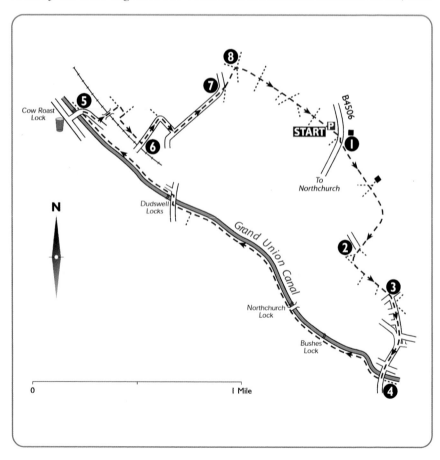

Cow Roast Lock

in those times this area was a hive of industry. In 1813 a bronze helmet, known as the Tring helmet, was found while digging the canal. It is now in the British Museum.

6. Turn left. Follow the lane round a right-hand bend to a T-junction. Turn left, signed 'Norcott Hill and Berkhamsted Common only'.

7. When the lane bends left at a small parking area, leave the lane to continue in the same direction into woodland on a signed bridleway.

8. Leave the wood at the far side and bear right to walk with woodland on the right and common on the left. Keep ahead on this line, which eventually leads back through a short stretch of woodland to the parking area where this walk started.

MARSWORTH RESERVOIRS

This is a waterside walk par excellence, encompassing four reservoirs and two branches of the Grand Union Canal, as well as a short stretch by the main canal. The reservoirs exist to provide water for the canal and are all managed as nature reserves. They are famous for their bird life, and all sorts of waterfowl are regularly to be seen. The route also climbs about 100 ft or so at one point and this gives excellent views of the scarp slope of the Chilterns and across the Vale of Aylesbury. Walkers are positively welcomed, and numerous noticeboards tell you about the many features of interest and the wildlife.

- **DISTANCE:** 4 miles
- **MAP:** OS Explorer 181 Chiltern Hills North
- **STARTING POINT:** Startop's car park, Marsworth (charge): GR 919141
- **HOW TO GET THERE:** Marsworth is on the B489 Aston Clinton–Dunstable road, about 2 miles north of its junction with the A41. The car park is at the south end of the village, more or less opposite the Angler's Retreat.
- **REFRESHMENTS:** You will not be short of opportunities for refreshments during the second half of this walk. It passes three pubs: the historic Half Moon in Wilstone (tel. 01442 826410), and the White Lion (tel. 01442 822325) and Angler's Retreat (tel. 01442 822250) in Marsworth, where this route starts and ends. Alternatively, there are two teashops. One at a farm shop (tel. 01442 828478) is just off the route, signed from the path by Wilstone reservoir and reached by a somewhat muddy and overgrown path starting down some steps. If you choose to visit it, you do not need to return to the reservoir but can turn left out of the teashop along the road and then turn right into Wilstone to pick up the route at point 9. The other, Bluebells (tel. 01442 891708), is by the canal at the end of the walk and has a pleasant outdoor seating area.

THE WALK

1. Take a track through a gate at the far end of the car park. Walk beside the canal for 50 yards and then bear right at a fork to walk beside a reservoir.

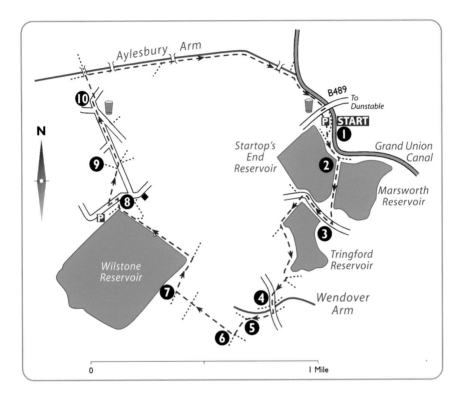

2. At the next junction turn right to walk between Startop's End and Marsworth reservoirs and follow this path to a lane.

3. Turn right, using the footway on the left-hand side. At the far end of Tringford Reservoir, on the left, bear left on a signed path to continue round the reservoir. Ignore a path on the right and continue ahead to reach a gate onto a track. Through the gate turn right along the track to continue in the same direction to a road.

4. Turn left, uphill, to a bridge over a canal, the Wendover arm of the Grand Union Canal. At the far side of the bridge turn right on a signed path beside the canal.

The Wendover arm (see walk 12, page 59) closed in 1904 because it was losing so much water. It is undergoing restoration in stages. This is possible because modern materials should be able to overcome the problems that defeated the canal in the 19th century. At the time of

Swans on Tringford Reservoir

writing, the first phase of restoration – construction of a short length of new channel, bridge, and winding hole to allow full-length boats to navigate to Little Tring – has been opened.

5. When the canal widens, turn left, away from the canal, to reach a small metal gate and cross-path.

6. Turn right, going through another small metal gate after a few yards, and walk along the right-hand side of two fields. Cross a canal (under restoration at the time of writing), using a wooden footbridge if necessary; then press on in the same direction to a cross-track.

7. Turn right for about 300 yards. When the trees beside the track end, turn left on a track and walk beside Wilstone Reservoir. At the end of the reservoir, go down a grassy bank onto a road.

A huge diversity of birds is to be seen on these reservoirs, which have been declared Sites of Special Scientific Interest. One distinctive species you may observe is the grey heron – poised beside the canals and reservoirs to catch a fish or seen as a large, broad-winged bird flapping slowly overhead. They build large nests in the small trees here at Wilstone Reservoir. By April the first scruffy chicks can be seen and by mid-summer the young birds, recognizable by their greyer plumage, join the adults in fishing.

8. Turn left and in 30 yards turn right over a stile and head diagonally right across a field to a stile, footbridge, and track. Cross the track and continue on the path to a lane.

9. Turn left through Wilstone.

In 1751, the Half Moon in Wilstone was the venue of the inquest into the death of Ruth Osborn, the climax of an outbreak of horrific mob violence in this area. Ruth and her husband, John, were both over 70 and dependent on charity for their living. They had been begging at a farm in nearby Gubblecote but were turned away empty-handed when Ruth was observed to mutter. Shortly afterwards the farmer accused them of being witches, saying they had made his cows ill and caused him to suffer from fits.

Feelings against the unfortunate couple ran high and it was decided to hold a trial by ducking. The Osborns were taken into Tring workhouse for their own protection but this was attacked by an angry mob – contemporary accounts speak of over 4,000 people – and they were then taken to the vestry of the church for sanctuary. Unable to find them at first, the mob smashed the windows and demolished part of the workhouse, seized the governor, and threatened to burn down the town! As the threat was very real, the poor couple were eventually given up to the mob and dragged to a pond at Wilstone, where they were tied in sacking and ducked under: Ruth was soon dead.

Despite so many people having been involved, the authorities met a wall of obstruction. Many who gave evidence said they did not know the people involved. One man was hanged for his part in the affair. A local chimney sweep, William Colley, who had apparently held Ruth under the water and then passed his cap round for contributions from the onlookers, was executed, with a detachment of over 100 soldiers present to make sure it happened. His body was left hanging in chains for years afterwards as a warning to the public of the dim view the authorities took of such events in those benighted times.

10. Just past the village hall and children's play area, turn left on a signed path along a track to a canal, the Aylesbury arm of the Grand Union Canal. Turn right along the towpath. Carry on beside the canal as it joins the main Grand Union Canal to Marsworth. At the White Lion, go up to the road. Turn right, back to the car park on the left where this walk started.

A branch canal to Aylesbury was first mooted in 1794, and the local traders were keen to be connected to a trade artery such as this. The problem was always the supply of water, and the scheme was not finally agreed until 1811. The arm opened in 1814 and was initially very busy, with substantial traffic in both directions. However, like all canals, it withered in the face of competition from the railway. Commercial traffic clung on until the 1960s and the last regular delivery of coal to Aylesbury was in 1964. Since then the canal's fortunes have been revived, after much effort by the Aylesbury Canal Society and other amenity bodies, for pleasure boating and other recreational uses.

The Aylesbury arm of the Grand Union Canal

WENDOVER WOODS AND CANAL

This route is among the more energetic in this book, with a long, steady climb through the glorious Wendover Woods to the highest point of the Chilterns. Your exertions are amply rewarded by some superb views across the Vale of Aylesbury. The views are at their best in winter when the trees are bare; so perhaps a sparkling clear day in winter is best for this excellent walk. On the other hand, the colours are magnificent in autumn, the flowers beautiful in spring, and the trees a delight in summer. Whenever you decide to do it, make sure it is a clear day to get the best from this delightful walk. The return leg is beside the Wendover arm of the Grand Union Canal. This has been closed for over a century but still carries water. Shaded by trees, it is rich in all sorts of waterfowl and you might even catch sight of the blue flash of a kingfisher. Arguably, this is the most attractive stretch of canal-side walking of all in this book and is strongly recommended.

- **DISTANCE:** 6 miles
- **MAP:** OS Explorer 181 Chiltern Hills North
- **STARTING POINT:** The end of the Wendover arm of the Grand Union Canal, on Wharf Road, Wendover: GR 869082
- **HOW TO GET THERE:** Wharf Road runs east from the B4009 towards Aylesbury, about 200 yards north of the centre of Wendover. It can also be accessed from the B4009 towards Tring and at this end it is called Manor Road, the name changing part way along.
- **REFRESHMENTS:** The Café in the Woods is just where you would wish for some refreshment after the exertion of the climb. It serves sandwiches, snacks, and excellent cakes and has tables inside and out. It is open every day from 9.30 am until 4.30 pm. There is no telephone. There are no pubs on this route.

THE WALK

1. Find the iron railings that mark the end of the canal. Facing up the canal, turn right (east) and walk to the main road. Turn left to pedestrian-controlled lights in 20 yards and cross the road to walk along Colet Road.

The Café in the Woods

2. Take the first left, Barlow Road. At the end of the road continue ahead on a public bridleway along a surfaced drive. When the drive ends at a house, bear right on a signed path to meet a cross-path after 40 yards. (Note: the path ahead at the cross-path leads straight up the hillside to join the route between points 4 and 5. The route described, though longer, is a gentler climb and much more scenic.)

3. Turn right. Follow this path along the edge of a wood and then round to the left as a major path joins on the right and continue for about ¼ mile to a path on the left.

4. Turn sharp left, almost back on yourself, and follow the path uphill. Passing a succession of excellent views, continue to a wooden barrier and a complex path junction just below the crest of the ridge.

This area has by no means always been as wooded as it is today. In prehistoric times the hill was crowned with a camp or fort. The banks and ditch, which enclosed an area of about 17 acres, still exist to some extent but are hard to see, as they are now smothered in vegetation. Many of the paths up the hill, including one we shall use later to go down the hill, have become sunken by centuries of use as people travelled between the farmland in the valley and the settlement on top. Later on there was a farm on the site.

5. Continue ahead on an obvious track, past a barbecue site and parking area, to the main car park and café.

6. At the end of the car park, turn left on the entrance road and follow it round a left-hand bend. As it starts to bend right, turn left along a sunken path with a wooden barrier at the start. Continue ahead downhill as a path joins on the left and, when it becomes a lane keep ahead to a main road.

7. Cross the road and continue ahead on a drive (do not be deterred by the Ministry of Defence sign). Immediately after a road on the right, turn right on a waymarked path to rejoin the drive further on. Continue along the drive, past extensive playing fields, with excellent views beyond.

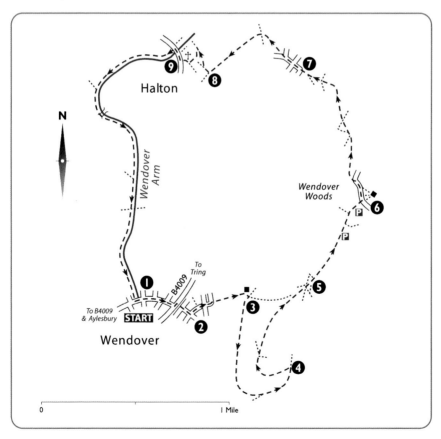

When the Rothschild family of banking fame settled in Buckinghamshire in the 19th century, they built seven magnificent mansions near Aylesbury and one of these was Halton. Alfred Rothschild inherited the estate in 1879 and immediately started to develop it into a pastoral paradise with velvet lawns and sweeping drives. He liked to view his estate from a small carriage pulled by a pair of zebras. The house, in which he

The path alongside the canal at point 9 of the walk

regularly welcomed royalty, high society, and many of the top entertainers of the day, was modelled on a French château. The Royal Flying Corps came to Halton in 1913, and the RAF bought the whole estate following the death of Alfred in 1918. The house, not visible on this walk but still apparently magnificent, is the officers' mess. RAF Halton has fulfilled many functions, especially in training airmen and women, and, until 1995, was the site of Princess Mary's RAF hospital.

8. Just after trees start on the right, turn right on a waymarked path. Bear slightly right on the main path for about 250 yards and then turn very sharp left, almost back on yourself, on a path signed by a waymark on a post. After about 50 yards, follow the path round to the right, to a gate into a churchyard. Walk through the churchyard to a road.

The churchyard is rather a sobering spot with many graves of RAF men who died before their time. The church looks as if it has been nailed together because of the little flints stuck in the mortar. It has a most attractive and unusual modern stained-glass window and, at the time of writing, serves teas on summer Sundays. The Rothschilds built most of the cottages in Halton for estate workers. It is worth taking a few moments to wander round and look at the unusual decorative plaques on several of the houses.

9. Turn right to a bridge over the canal. Immediately over the bridge turn left on a path beside the canal and follow this back to the start.

CHENIES AND THE CHESS VALLEY

This outstanding walk encompasses all that is best about the Chilterns and illustrates why it is such a great area to explore on foot. It starts on the side of the Chess valley, where a high level path leads to Chenies. Though much of this path is in woodland, there is an open section with wonderful views over the Chess valley to be explored later. Chenies is very picturesque and complete with a manor house, church, village green – and two pubs. The route then drops down through attractive woodland to the valley and an opportunity to buy some of the watercress for which the Chess valley is famous. A path then leads along the valley bottom, never too far from the river, before a final climb through more woodland back to the start.

- **DISTANCE:** 5 miles
- **MAP:** OS Explorer 172 Chiltern Hills East
- **STARTING POINT:** Stony Lane parking area, Little Chalfont: GR 005982
- **HOW TO GET THERE:** From the A404 between Amersham and Rickmansworth, at the extreme eastern edge of Little Chalfont, turn north along Stony Lane, signed 'Latimer 1, Flaunden 2½', to the parking area on the left after about 400 yards.
- **REFRESHMENTS:** There are two pubs in Chenies, the Bedford Arms (tel. 01923 283301) and the Red Lion (tel. 01923 282722), both passed on the route.

THE WALK

1. Cross the road and take a bridleway along a track opposite, initially along the top edge of a wood. Continue along the track when it leaves the wood. When the track bears slightly right as you approach a house, keep ahead through a wooden kissing gate on a path through woodland, and follow the path as it bears left after 50 yards.

2. At the end of the wood turn right along a cross-path up into Chenies, to emerge by the gates of Chenies Manor.

Chenies (pronounced Chainies) used to be called Isenhampstead. In the Middle Ages the manor was owned by the Cheyne family and

63

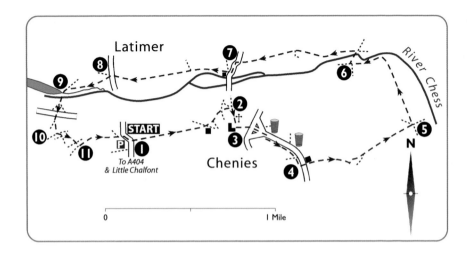

eventually the earlier name was dropped. The manor passed to the Russell family in 1526. The Russells became the earls and dukes of Bedford in 1550. They rebuilt the manor house and created the family mausoleum in the adjacent church. All the Russells are buried there, from the first earl onwards, and it is said that this is the best collection of funeral monuments in any parish church in England but we ordinary mortals may only peep at it through the glass partition. More information about the church is given in the very comprehensive booklet available within. Death duties forced the Russells to sell Chenies after the death of the twelfth duke in 1954, though they had long since moved to Woburn Abbey. Henry VIII visited Chenies Manor twice and Elizabeth I paid three visits while it was still the main Russell residence. The manor is open to the public from 2 pm to 5 pm on Wednesday and Thursday between April and October and all Bank Holiday Mondays. Tel. 01494 762888.*

3. Turn left down the drive to the village green. Cross the green and go ahead out of the village on a road signed 'Chorleywood 1¾, Rickmansworth 4', passing the Bedford Arms and Red Lion pubs.

4. Immediately after a red-brick house with numerous chimneys, turn left through a small wooden gate on the Chilterns Way. Follow the waymarked path gently downhill through woods, across a field, and through more woods to a gate at the bottom of the woods.

5. Go through the gate and turn left on a cross-path, signed 'Chenies 1¼ m', soon re-entering woodland. Follow the path through the woods, with the first glimpses of the Chess on the right, to a surfaced track.

The clear water of the Chess, bubbling out of the chalk at a constant 10°C, provides ideal conditions for growing watercress, which used to be cultivated all along the valley. One farm remains and you can buy the watercress, if you are willing to carry quite a large bundle!

6. Turn right to a footbridge over the Chess. Some 20 yards after crossing the bridge turn left between metal barriers onto a boardwalk. Continue along this path as it turns right, away from the river, leading through woodland and then across water meadows to a lane.

As the path turns away from the river it skirts round Frogmore Meadow. Water meadows are often drained, have been ploughed up and replanted with modern strains of grass, and had fertilizer and pesticides used on them. This makes them much less valuable for wildlife, and so areas where this has never happened are important

A footbridge over the River Chess

relics; *Frogmore Meadow is one such. It is owned and managed by the local wildlife trust and there is an access point at the far side of the meadow, some 25 yards to the left of the path. It has many species of flowering plants and is alive with all manner of insects feeding on them in summer, but be warned: it can be marshy!*

7. Turn left for 120 yards; then turn right through metal farm gates, passing to the right of a house, to walk beside a branch of the Chess. Ignore a path on the right and keep ahead on this path to a lane.

Neptune guards the Chess here

8. Cross the lane to find two signed paths starting through a wooden kissing gate. Take the path bearing half left to walk beside perhaps the most open and attractive stretch of the Chess, to a gate onto a surfaced drive.

The imposing house you can see up the hill is Latimer House. The Chess has been dammed here to create an artificial lake and, on the right of the drive, the waterfall with the statue of Neptune. The house is now a conference centre.

9. Turn left. When the drive shortly forks, go through a kissing gate ahead and slightly right across a field to a road. Cross the road and continue on the path for 20 yards. Now fork left to walk next to the fence on the left to a kissing gate into a wood.

10. Immediately through the gate take the second path to the left. When the path forks after 20 yards, take the left, less steep, fork and climb through the wood to a T-junction with a cross-path just inside the wood.

11. Turn left and follow the path to a lane. Turn right along the lane, back to the start.

WALK 14

CHESHAM AND THE RIVER CHESS

Chesham sprawls across the head of the Chess valley. This route climbs quickly out of the town to explore the hills on its northern side. The climb is steep but the reward is a series of excellent views before the route descends into the valley. Surprisingly, the route returns to the centre of Chesham with very little town road walking, thanks to a great riverside path.

- **DISTANCE:** 6 miles
- **MAPS:** OS Explorer 181 Chiltern Hills North and 172 Chiltern Hills East
- **STARTING POINT:** Chesham station. This is the end of one branch of the London Underground Metropolitan line and there is an adjacent car park (charge): GR 960016
- **HOW TO GET THERE:** Chesham is on the A416 Amersham–Berkhamsted road. From the A416 in Chesham, take the road signed 'Ley Hill 2, Station'. The car park is on the left before the station.
- **REFRESHMENTS:** The pub at Tylers Hill, shown on the OS map, has gone the way of so many other country pubs in this area of hugely inflated property prices and is now a private house. This means there is no source of refreshment on the walk until the very end, where there is the venerable George and Dragon and a couple of teashops on Chesham High Street.

THE WALK

Chesham has been a market town since the time of the Saxons, and relics spanning the thousands of years from the Stone Age to the Romans suggest there has been a settlement here as long as people have lived in the Chilterns. The modern town grew with the arrival of the railway in 1889, and this is the final north-westerly outpost of the Metropolitan line.

1. Take a signed path to the right of the station. Turn left on the first path, crossing the railway line. At the far side of the bridge, turn right. At the end of some old railings on the left, turn very sharp left, more or less back on yourself. When level with the bridge again, turn right and climb steeply uphill, to a stile into a field. Continue ahead across the

Chesham High Street

field, pausing at the top of the hill to admire the panoramic views.

2. At the far side of the field go through a metal kissing-gate and immediately turn left through a second kissing gate to walk along the left-hand side of a field to a gate at the far end. Through this gate turn right on a fenced path leading into a field.

3. Turn left across the field. Cross a track and continue ahead along the left-hand side of the field. In the next field bear slightly right. At the end of this field follow the path down into a dip, across a track, and up the other side to meet a cross-track at the top of the hill.

4. Turn left to walk along the right-hand side of a field. At the end of the field do not go through the metal kissing-gate but bear slightly right to walk along the left-hand side of three fields to a stile onto a track.

5. Turn right and almost immediately bear right on the drive to Cowcroft Farm. Pass the entrance to the farm and keep ahead on a track.

6. Soon after a left-hand bend, turn right along a track. Bear left when the track forks to eventually meet a cross-path at the edge of the wood.

7. Turn right and continue for about ¼ mile.

8. Turn right through a small gate on a waymarked path. Follow the path across the field to find a gate at the bottom right-hand corner giving on to a fenced cross-path.

9. Turn left and follow this path to emerge on a concrete drive. Keep ahead to a lane.

10. Turn right. When the lane bends left by a cottage, go over a stile to continue on a signed path in the same direction across a field to a stile by a gate. Bear half right across a second field to find a stile that, at the time of writing, is rather overgrown, though quite sound.

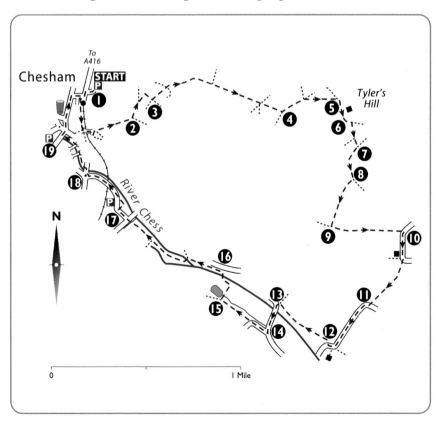

11. Turn right along a lane and follow this down into the Chess Valley past the entrance to Blackwell Farm.

12. Some 40 yards after the farm entrance, turn right, signed 'Chess Valley Walk', along what looks like an entrance drive. Follow the path round to the left to a stile. Over the stile continue ahead along the left-hand side of two fields to a stile.

13. Over the stile turn left to a road and go left along the road for 200 yards.

14. Turn right along Holloway Lane, walking with a branch of the Chess on the right. When the road bends left, continue ahead in the same direction, again signed 'Chess Valley Walk'.

15. Watch for a metal kissing-gate on the right, immediately before a tall metal mesh fence starts on the right. Go through the kissing gate and follow the path to a bridge over the river, just before a road.

The Chess Valley was an important area for growing watercress (see walk 13, page 65) and the works on the left bottling Chilterns water is on the site of old watercress beds.

16. Immediately over the bridge, turn left on a riverside path. At a weir cross to the other bank and press on by the water, initially between two branches of the river. When the way ahead is barred by houses, bear left by a small branch of the river to a footbridge and a road.

17. Cross the road and go ahead along Moor Road. When the houses on the right (Shantung Terrace) end, turn right on a path back to the river. Turn left to walk with the river on your right, rejoining the road and going under the railway to a main road at a roundabout.

18. Cross the road and turn right; in 20 yards, bear left on a signed path to carry on by the river. Stay on the right bank.

19. When this path ends at a road, turn right. Cross the main road and continue along the pedestrianized High Street. Turn right up Station Road, back to the station.

LITTLE MISSENDEN AND THE RIVER MISBOURNE

The route uses an ancient sunken path to climb from the pretty village of Little Missenden, with excellent views glimpsed through the hedge as you climb. A lovely woodland path leads back to the Misbourne valley and a path beside Shardeloes Lake and the river guides you back to Little Missenden. Humphrey Repton, who laid out the grounds of Shardeloes House, described it as 'one of the most beautiful situations in England', and I think you will agree. The path shows the Chilterns at their best, with views of the rolling hills crowned with woods.

- **DISTANCE:** 4 miles
- **MAP:** OS Explorer 172 Chiltern Hills East
- **STARTING POINT:** The Crown, Little Missenden: GR 926988
- **HOW TO GET THERE:** Turn off the A413 Amersham–Aylesbury road, on a minor road through Little Missenden. Park on the roadside near the Crown, which is at the east end of the village.
- **REFRESHMENTS:** The Crown (tel. 01494 862571) in Little Missenden, where this route starts and finishes, is the only source of refreshment en route. It has a pretty garden with its own serving hatch. At lunchtime it offers a good selection of sandwiches, salads, and ploughman's.

THE WALK

Little Missenden, having been bypassed by the railway, escaped the advance of Metroland that had such a profound influence on much of this part of the Chilterns. It is everyone's idea of what an English village should be, with an ancient church, a manor house, and old coaching inns grouped together to charming effect, and it has been the backdrop to several episodes of Midsomer Murders. *The church, near the centre of the village, is of no great architectural merit, but is worth exploring because of its great age. It is said that the most recent addition is the porch added in 1450. It was founded by the Saxons, but has some Roman bricks in the chancel arch. Perhaps the most interesting features are the wall paintings. These brightly-coloured pictures were usual in medieval churches, where most of the congregation was*

71

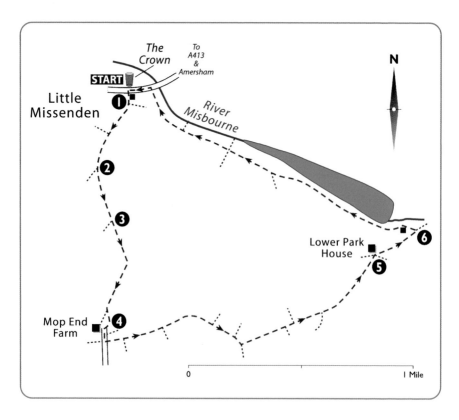

illiterate. Later, in Puritan times, they fell from fashion and were painted over, and the majority have been lost. A few, like these, remain to give us a glimpse into the past.

One resident of Little Missenden was Dr Bates, who lived in the manor house by the church. He was doctor to Francis Dashwood of West Wycombe and the longest survivor of the Hell Fire Club (see walk 4, page 24). It certainly didn't do him any harm, as he lived to be 98. To the end of his life he maintained that the stories were fabrications.

1. Almost opposite the Crown take an unsurfaced track past Toby's Lane Farm. When the track bends left at the end of the house, continue in the same direction on a path.

It is worth taking a closer look at some of the trees bordering the path. They were planted as a hedge, which was originally maintained by being laid. This means the branches are partly cut through and bent so that they lie horizontally, and this encouraged them to grow as a thick hedge that could be cut to the required height. At some point the hedge was no longer maintained in this way and so the plants have grown into full-sized trees but they retain the evidence of their early treatment in the way they grow.

2. Some 40 yards after a wood starts on the right, fork left to continue along the left-hand side of the wood. When the wood on the right ends, continue with a field on the right for about 250 yards. As the path bends right, watch for a stile on the left.

3. Cross the stile. The path is not usually apparent on the ground. It goes diagonally right to a hedge gap (though it may be easier to walk round the edge of the field). It then continues in the same direction across the next field. At the edge of the field, turn right to walk with a hedge on the left. As a track leading to Mop End Farm starts, go over a stile on the left and bear right across the field to find a stile just to the left of the farm buildings.

4. Over the stile continue along the lane in the same direction for 100 yards and then turn left on a signed public footpath. Follow this path through woods, gently downhill, to arrive at two stiles. Cross the stile on the left to walk along the right-hand side of a field. At the end of the field join a track. Carry on along the track, ignoring a track on the left after 50 yards. Bear left at a fork to walk – with a field on the left and a line of trees on the right – towards a cream-coloured house. The path ends at the drive to Shardeloes House at Lower Park House.

Shardeloes Lake

5. Turn right along the drive.

6. Turn left on a signed public footpath at the far side of the cricket pitch. Follow the track round

The River Misbourne

behind the pavilion and then bear right to a gate. Follow the path and track by the lake and the River Misbourne (see Walk 17, page 80), back to Little Missenden.

The large white house on the hill is Shardeloes. It was the home of the Drake family. In 1602 Joan Tothill, the eldest of the 33 children of William Tothill of Shardeloes, was forced against her will to marry Francis Drake of Esher. From this unhappy union descended the Drake family who dominated Amersham and controlled the rotten borough for over 200 years. Legend has it that a curse befell the family, stopping any direct heir from inheriting the family wealth, the curse having been placed by the family of a boy murdered at sea whilst in the Drake family employ.

The present house was built in the mid-18th century. It was requisitioned as a maternity home at the outbreak of the Second World War so that Londoners could escape the horrors of the bombing to give birth in the peace of the Chilterns: over 5,000 children were born here. After the war it fell into disrepair and was bought by a property company which planned to demolish the house and redevelop the site. After a long battle, its architectural merit and historical importance were recognized and a preservation order was placed on it, preventing the demolition. The house was restored and converted into flats and houses.

The grounds and the park, were laid out by landscape architect Humphrey Repton in 1793, utilizing elements of the earlier landscaped grounds. The lake is not natural but was created by damming the River Misbourne.

HUGHENDEN VALLEY

The valleys of the Chilterns were carved by run-off from the ice sheet during the last Ice Age, when this area was not covered by glaciers but was permanently frozen tundra. Many of the valleys are dry today and Hughenden valley is quite unusual because it has a stream – you could not call it a river – that flows most of the time in its lower reaches. This pleasant walk climbs up the east side of the valley to Cryers Hill and then descends into the valley itself. Much of the way is along wooded paths, with the occasional lovely view of the valley below and the hills beyond. The return along the valley floor, beside the stream, is charming, and about half is through parkland, where the green expanses of the valley are decorated with many magnificent trees.

- **DISTANCE:** 4 miles
- **MAP:** OS Explorer 172 Chiltern Hills East
- **STARTING POINT:** The car park opposite 274 Hughenden Road, High Wycombe: GR 865944
- **HOW TO GET THERE:** Hughenden Road is the A4128 High Wycombe–Prestwood road. The car park is on the edge of High Wycombe and is not signed.
- **REFRESHMENTS:** The White Lion (tel. 01494 712303) at Cryers Hill is a friendly pub with a pleasant garden that serves food at lunchtime and is well positioned about 50 yards off the route, about halfway round. The National Trust tearoom at Hughenden Manor (tel. 01494 755576) is excellent and can be combined with a visit to the house but is about ¼ mile off the route, uphill at the end of point 9.

THE WALK

1. Return to the road and turn left along the footway on the left-hand side. When this leaves the roadside and becomes a surfaced path, continue ahead for about 150 yards.

2. Cut up to the busy road and cross it to find a signed path starting up some steps. Go through a kissing gate at the top of the steps and continue up the right-hand side of the field as far as a gate on the right. Go through the gate and ahead for 10 yards to a cross-path.

An inviting picnic spot

3. Turn left along the path and continue gently uphill through a narrow band of trees to a T-junction.

4. Turn left into Millfield Wood Nature Reserve and follow the path through the wood, ignoring two paths to the left and passing an information board telling you something about the ecology of this wood. Go over a stile out of the wood and bear half right to a stile onto a track.

5. Turn left along the track to a road.

6. Turn left along the road and continue for about ¾ mile to the main road in Cryers Hill. (The White Lion is 50 yards to the right at the junction.)

Watch out as you walk past the cemetery. Travellers at this spot have apparently been startled by the appearance of a ghostly Green Man, the traditional English spirit of the woods.

7. Turn left, signed 'Hughenden, 1 High Wycombe 2½' ; in about 120 yards, bear right along a surfaced drive. Bear left when this forks after about 50 yards. When the drive ends, bear right on a fenced footpath starting over a stile and follow it down to a kissing gate onto a cross-path.

8. Turn left and continue ahead when this becomes first a drive and then a lane to the main road through Hughenden Valley village.

The Hughenden stream

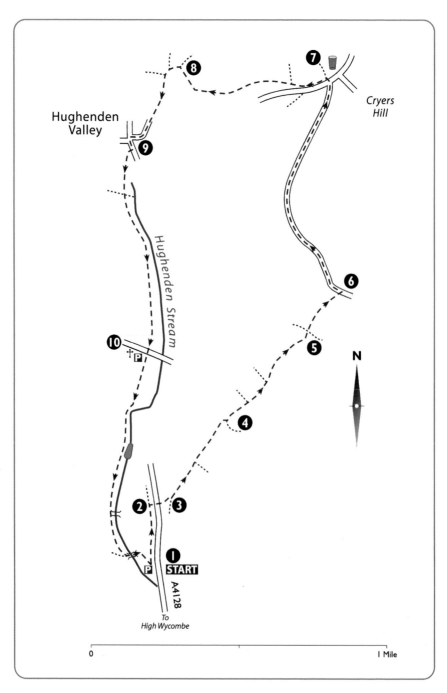

Cryers
Hill

Hughenden
Valley

Hughenden Stream

N

START

A4128

To
High Wycombe

0   I Mile

9. Turn left and in 50 yards turn right onto a signed path that starts up three steps and then immediately turns left. Follow the path into a field, across that field, and along the right-hand side of three further fields to the drive to Hughenden Manor.

The Hughenden stream starts near where you crossed the main road in Hughenden Valley village. The name has had many spellings over the centuries but one, Hitchenden, suggests Celtic origins as the word hitchen *means 'dried-up stream' in Celtic; so this implies it has always been a fickle stream. However, like many watercourses in the Chilterns, its flow has reputedly diminished in recent times, probably due to over-abstraction of ground water from the aquifer that feeds it. Apparently Disraeli caught a large trout in the stream and that doesn't look likely today. The stream flows south through Hughenden Park to High Wycombe, where it joins the River Wye.*

10. Cross the drive below the car park and to the left of the church. Continue ahead down the valley on no clear path, soon walking with the stream on your left. In sight of the car park, bear left over a bridge and follow a surfaced path back to the car park where this walk started.

Coins and pottery have been found round here, showing that the Romans recognized a good place to live. Hughenden Manor is mentioned in the Domesday Book, *but is now best known as the home of Benjamin Disraeli, who was brought up over the hill at Bradenham. He loved the Chilterns and acquired the estate as his home in 1848, for £35,000. There has been a church here since the 12th century but not much remains of the old structure, as it was extensively restored in Disraeli's time. He is buried in the churchyard in the family vault. There is a memorial plaque in the church, placed there by his most famous admirer, 'his grateful and affectionate sovereign and friend, Victoria R.I', who visited Hughenden several times. The National Trust acquired the house and 190 acres of parkland in 1946, and the park is shared with Wycombe District Council. The house is open to the public Wednesday to Saturday and on Bank Holiday Mondays, from 2 pm till 6 pm, between April and October; and at weekends in March (tel. 01494 532580). The house is at the top of the hill and can be reached by going right up the drive. There is a good tearoom in the old stables to reward you for your efforts if you do decide to climb up to visit it.*

THE SOURCE OF THE RIVER MISBOURNE

The main question of this route is whether it will be a waterside walk at all! The upper section of the Misbourne is a 'winterbourne' – one of the 'now you see it, now you don't' rivers of chalk hills. It lies above the lower limit of the water table and below its upper limit; so whether it flows or not depends on the state of the aquifer beneath. Usually the water table is higher in winter but the Misbourne is historically very erratic. It has been known to flow during droughts and dry up in wet seasons! This is most likely to be a waterside walk at the end of a wet winter but nothing can be guaranteed. It is a great route at any time of year, though, and includes the reputed source of the Misbourne, as well as typical Chiltern scenery comprising a patchwork of woods and fields, and some fine views.

- **DISTANCE:** 4½ miles
- **MAP:** OS Explorer 181 Chiltern Hills North
- **STARTING POINT:** Great Missenden car park, Link Road (charge): GR 894014
- **HOW TO GET THERE:** Great Missenden lies just off the A413 Amersham–Wendover road. The car park is on the right of the road, linking the village to the main road.
- **REFRESHMENTS:** The Black Horse (tel. 01494 862537) overlooking Mobwell Pond serves food and is passed shortly after the start of the walk. It is the only source of refreshment directly on the route, but there are several pubs and restaurants in Great Missenden, where this walk starts.

THE WALK

1. Go to the rear of the car park and turn right on a path in front of high railings.

The path crosses the Misbourne at this point. It may have water in it to the left but is culverted to the right, which tells us something about the importance Great Missenden has attached to its river in the past.

Go over a stile and bear round to the left to a second stile. Press on across a field, soon walking by a channel, which is the bed of the Misbourne. Keep to the right of the river to find a stile about 50 yards from the far right corner of the field. Bear slightly left across the next field, towards the Black Horse pub and a road.

2. Turn right and in 50 yards turn left onto a path to the left of the entrance to Town End Farm, passing Mobwell Pond on your left. Follow the path under a railway arch to a gate. Through the gate bear left to a road.

The Misbourne is said to rise at this pond and it stretches 14 miles south-east to the Colne (see Walk 8, page 43) near Uxbridge. However, it has been known to rise above this point, at Rignall Farm and, before the First World War, there are records of the farm kitchen having to be pumped out.

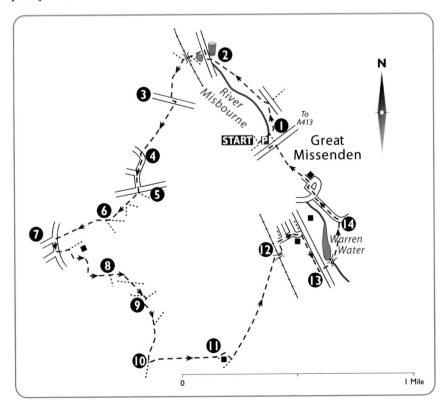

81

3. Turn left and in 20 yards turn right over a stile by a gate. Walk up the left-hand side of two fields and then ahead on a fenced path to a road.

4. Turn left to a T-junction with a main road.

5. Cross the road to a path into a wood and immediately turn right on a signed path. Stay on the waymarked path, ignoring paths on the left, to reach an obvious cross-path.

6. Turn right to shortly leave the wood, and carry on along the path up to a road.

7. Turn left, and then left again in 85 yards onto the drive to Andlows Farm. After 100 yards, when the hedge on the right ends, turn right through a gate. Through a second gate follow the path to the left, round the edge of a field and into a wood.

8. The correct path through the wood is not obvious but is waymarked by white arrows on trees; so watch for these. Ignore a path on the right, 15 yards into the wood, and continue ahead for 120 yards. Now turn right on a waymarked path and follow this path to a gate onto a clear cross-track.

9. Turn right and follow the track to a surfaced drive.

10. Turn left along the drive. As the drive approaches a building, bear left to stay on the drive.

11. Just before reaching large double gates, turn left through a gap in the fence and walk over to a gate giving onto a track. Follow the track down into a dip and up the other side to a gate. Press on ahead over a railway bridge to another gate.

12. Turn right through this gate and walk down a road. At the end of the road turn right to the entrance to Misbourne School and immediately left. At the end of this short road turn right on a footpath between the school grounds and the main road and continue for about 250 yards.

13. Turn left at the first real gap to the main road. Cross the road and

Mobwell Pond

take a footpath along a track opposite, signed 'South Bucks Way'. At the end of the track go through a metal kissing-gate into Missenden Abbey parkland and ahead a few yards to meet the River Misbourne again, which may be dry or flowing rapidly. Cross the river, using the stylish bridge if necessary, and bear half left to find a wooden kissing-gate and some steps.

The stretch of water beyond the bridge is Warren Water, constructed as an ornamental lake for Missenden Abbey, the building overlooking the lake. It was founded by William de Missenden in 1133. James Oldham, a London ironmonger, bought the decayed estate in 1787 and constructed the building we see today. It incorporates a few traces of the original monastery and is now used as a residential study centre.

14. At the top of the steps turn left along a lane. At a junction at a small green, turn right and almost immediately left to take a signed path starting along a lane to the left of school buildings. Follow this by a park to a road and the car park. The Misbourne lies in a culvert beneath this park. It has been suggested that it could be opened up again, if the flow improves with the rescue plan.

THE GADE VALLEY

It always seems to me that the north-eastern Chilterns do not receive the same interest as the hills further west and this is a shame because they are just as much a part of the Area of Outstanding Natural Beauty and deserve more attention. This short walk is a splendid introduction to this attractive area, exploring part of the valley of the River Gade and the hills, woods and fields around Great Gaddesden.

The River Gade at the start of the walk

- **DISTANCE:** 3½ miles
- **MAP:** OS Explorer 182 St Albans and Hatfield
- **STARTING POINT:** Great Gaddesden Garden Centre car park, whose owners are happy for walkers to use it. Do pay attention to closing times, when the gates are locked: for example, it closes at 4.30 pm on Sunday: GR 031113
- **HOW TO GET THERE:** From the A4146, Hemel Hempstead–Leighton Buzzard road, about 3 miles north of Hemel Hempstead, take a minor road signed 'Great Gaddesden ½' to the garden centre on the right.
- **REFRESHMENTS:** There is no source of refreshment on this walk.

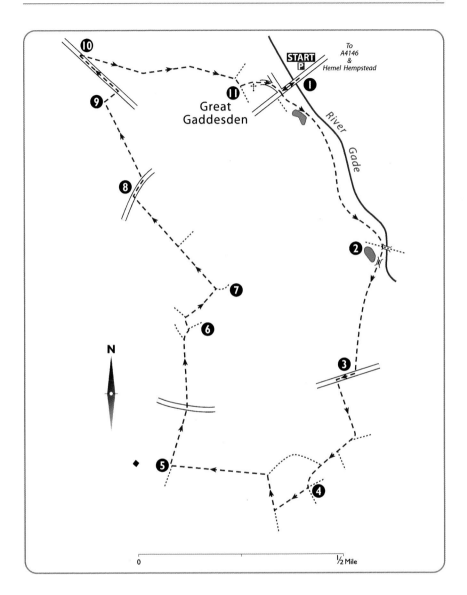

THE WALK

1. From the entrance to the garden centre car park, turn right along the lane. Some 15 yards after Church Meadows on the right, turn left over a stile. Note that this is not the signed footpath to the right, which you will need to use if the water meadows are flooded. Bear left to pass between the river and a pretty pond. There is no defined path, as

85

this is open access land, but make your way across the meadow by the river, perhaps cutting off a loop, as far as a second pond.

2. Do not go over the footbridge over the river but stay on the right-hand bank, crossing a small footbridge over the outlet of the pond. Go ahead to a stile as the river bends left. Over the stile, go ahead to find in the far right corner of the field a metal kissing-gate onto a lane.

The church at Great Gaddesden

3. Turn right and, in 80 yards, turn left through a wooden kissing-gate on a signed path and follow this up the field to a wood. Continue on the path as it bears right through the wood, ignoring all side paths, to a junction of paths and a track at the far edge of the wood.

4. Turn right on a signed path across a field to a cross-path in 200 yards. Turn right and in 150 yards turn left on a cross-path heading towards a farm house and buildings in the valley.

The stately home you can see on top of the hill across the valley is Gaddesden Place, which was gutted by fire on 1st February 1905, destroying thousands of pounds worth of valuable paintings, furniture, and heirlooms, though some items were rescued, including cases of drink from the wine cellar. The fire originated in a beam and lath and plaster work surrounding a section of flue piping. A smell of burning had been noticed for days but, despite rigorous searches, no cause had been found. The blaze sprang to life in the early hours of the morning. A servant rode the three miles to Hemel Hempstead to alert the fire brigade, which quickly attended, but with no ready water supply nearby they were unable to quench the flames that had already taken a good hold on three or four rooms. In the aftermath of the blaze it was thought that the cellar was safe, although the house was in ruins.

Some staff were returning bottles to the cellar when a wall collapsed and smashed through the hall floor, burying the butler and a footman in red-hot bricks and debris. Sadly, they later died from their injuries.

5. Before reaching the farm, turn right beside the fence in front to a lane. Cross the lane and continue up the field on the opposite side towards a wood and a welcome seat, from which to admire the view. Continue on the path through the wood for 25 yards to a fork.

6. Bear left to reach a cross-path after 75 yards, near the edge of the wood. Turn right inside the wood and continue for about 200 yards.

7. Turn left out of the wood on a waymarked path. Go ahead to the left of a hedge to a lane.

8. Turn right; then turn left after 90 yards onto a signed path that leads along the right-hand side of a field and then right, along a narrow fenced path to a lane.

9. Turn left.

10. Some 30 yards after the entrance to the Buddhist centre, turn right on a path signed 'Great Gaddesden ½'. Follow this lovely path down the fields from kissing gate to kissing gate to arrive at two gates by the churchyard.

The Amaravati Buddhist Centre is a monastery with a resident community of monks and nuns. They follow the Theravada version of Buddhism from south-east Asia and welcome visitors who come on retreat. The monastery has been here for over 20 years.

11. Go through the gate on the right and shortly turn left to walk through the churchyard to a lane. Follow the lane to the right to a T-junction and turn left back to the car park where this walk started.

Nobody knows how long there has been a church on this spot, but the Domesday Book mentions that the re was a priest here in 1086. The present building suggests dates from the 12th century, and there are some Roman bricks and tiles incorporated in the building, presumably reused from older structures in the area.

TWO LAKES WALK

Langley Park and Black Park are twin country parks and each has an ornamental lake. This easy route explores them both and is almost completely level. Much of the walk is through woodland, and there is the added bonus of a superb view towards the end as the route crosses Temple Gardens, where the rhododendrons are at their best in May.

- **DISTANCE:** 4 miles
- **MAP:** OS Explorer 172 Chiltern Hills East
- **STARTING POINT:** Langley Park car park, Billet Lane (charge): GR 016821
- **HOW TO GET THERE:** Billet Lane leads south from the A412 Slough–Denham road, about ¼ mile west of Five Points roundabout at the junction of the A412 and A4007.
- **REFRESHMENTS:** The café at Black Park is ideally positioned about halfway round the walk and overlooks the lake. It has plenty of tables outside to enjoy the view and serves full meals and snacks as well as a selection of cakes and ice creams.

THE WALK

Note: Please be aware that Buckinghamshire County Council, which manages Langley Park and Black Park, is planning a major programme of renovation in Langley Park. This may affect signing and the crossing of the A412 and Temple Gardens, visited at the end of the walk, in particular, but it should not materially affect the route.

Langley Park and Black Park are both part of the Langley Park Estate. The first record dates from 1202, when King John granted Richard Montfitchet '100 live does and bucks out of his forest of Windsor to stock his park'. It seems likely that the park was already established by this time and was part of the forests of Wradisbury, hunted in by Saxon kings. The words 'park' and 'forest' in this context do not have the meaning conjured up today but refer to areas set aside for hunting by the nobility. The park remained essentially a royal park in the gift of the monarch. It was an attractive hunting property in close proximity to London and Windsor, and Henry VIII lived at Langley for a time. In 1551 the park was granted to the 18-year-old Princess Elizabeth by her brother, Edward VI.

1. Go through the gap in the wooden rail at the rear of the car park and turn left along a path to a complex path junction immediately after a gate across the path.

2. Take the second left, signed 'Beeches Way', for 25 yards; then turn right and continue for ½ mile.

3. Turn right through a metal kissing-gate opposite a gate with stone lions on the gate posts.

4. Some 100 yards after a footbridge and gate, at a notice about grazing land, turn right on a permissive path, shortly to walk beside the first of today's lakes.

Charles Spencer, 3rd Duke of Marlborough, bought Langley in 1738 to get away from living at Windsor with his grandmother, the redoubtable Sarah. He inherited Blenheim, the main seat of the Marlboroughs, in 1744, but Langley remained an attractive property for the family, situated between London and Blenheim and convenient for Windsor. He commissioned Stiff Leadbetter, who also built Shardeloes (passed on walk 15), to build a stylish and fashionable mansion. The 3rd Duke died in 1757 before the house was completed. His son George, 4th Duke of Marlborough, commissioned Lancelot 'Capability' Brown to produce proposals for landscaping Blenheim and, almost incidentally, it seems, to be responsible for much of what we see at Langley. This lake had

Black Park Lake

already been dug but as a straight and formal canal. Brown remodelled it into a sinuous shape in line with the fashions of the day. As an artificial feature, the lake would gradually become overgrown if left to itself, as it is showing signs of doing at the time of writing. Some restoration work to the lake is planned as part of the renovations.

5. At the end of the lake go through a gate and turn right along a track to the tarmac drive to Langley Park House. Turn left to walk on a path to the right of the drive to the entrance gates.

In 1788 the 4th Duke of Marlborough sold the estate to Robert Bateson Harvey, whose family retained the property until after the Second World War. During the war the house was first the south-east regional headquarters of the Home Guard and in 1944 the headquarters of Polish units preparing for D Day. Black Park was used as the location of a series of bomb dumps. Under the Green Belt (London and Home Counties) Act 1938, the county councils around London were empowered to purchase land to prevent the outward sprawl of London, and Buckinghamshire County Council bought the estate in 1945. Most of the estate is managed as the country parks we see today while the rest is let to farmers. The house is leased as a business headquarters and is not open to the public.

6. Cross the dual carriageway and turn right. In 70 yards, turn left on a surfaced drive and continue ahead on a track through a gate to a cross-track. Turn left to the café overlooking the Black Park Lake.

7. Turn left, then right, and right again to walk round the lake. At the far end of the lake continue round to the right to stay by the lake.

8. At the next path junction go ahead, away from the lake, signed 'open space heathland'. Follow the path round to the right: do not go ahead across a grassy area.

9. Some 10 yards after a finger-post sign for the café and lake to the right, bear left on a small woodland path, taking a left fork after 15 yards. The path passes a small pit on the right and then bears left and becomes much broader. Press on in the same direction over a track to reach a T-junction.

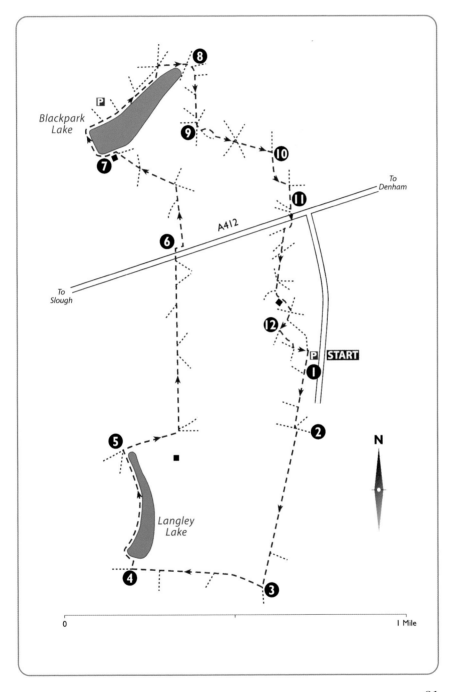

Blackpark
Lake

To
Denham

A412

To
Slough

START

N

Langley
Lake

0   I Mile

Langley Lake

10. Turn right to reach a cross-track. Turn right again to the main road.

11. Cross the road to find the start of a path. Walk along this for 50 yards to a fork. Bear left. Keep ahead as a faint path forks right after 100 yards and go over a cross-path after a further 25 yards. Press on along this path for another 150 yards to a fork. Bear slightly right, and then left at the next fork, after a further 30 yards, soon passing some ancient yews and then a terrace with a superb view to Windsor Castle. Follow this path round to the right, ignoring several smaller paths to left and right.

Over the years, of course, many changes were made to the gardens and they came to include several interesting features, so much so that Langley Park is included in English Heritage's Register of Parks and Gardens of Special Historic Interest. Sadly, in recent times they have become rather neglected, but all this is, we hope, about to change with the aid of lottery money. The terrace once had an Indian-style 'temple' from which to enjoy the wonderful view to Windsor. The restoration plan is to erect a new structure on the site. The rhododendrons are considered to be a magnificent collection, and it is planned to bring them back to their full glory, as well as making it easier to appreciate the many unusual shrubs and trees in the arboretum.

12. When the way ahead is barred by a gate, turn left and in about 100 yards turn left again at a cross-path back to the car park.

BURNHAM BEECHES

Burnham Beeches are over 500 acres of ancient woodland that are protected as a national nature reserve. Their importance is recognized for the many very ancient beech and oak trees to be found here and this route passes several, including the most venerable of all. Two streams cross the area, one of which has been dammed to make attractive ponds, and this walk visits both streams, the ponds, and The Mire, an important area of acid wetland. There is also an opportunity to see the phenomenon of swilly holes. The woods are beautiful at all times of the year and this short walk is one to enjoy and repeat many times.

- **DISTANCE:** 2½ miles
- **MAP:** OS Explorer 172 Chiltern Hills East
- **STARTING POINT:** Burnham Beeches Visitor Centre: GR 954850
- **HOW TO GET THERE:** At Farnham Common on the A355 Beaconsfield–Slough road, turn along Beeches Road, signed 'Burnham Beeches 1'. At the crossroads continue in the same direction along Lord Mayor's Drive. There are several parking bays on the left before the visitor centre, also on the left.
- **REFRESHMENTS:** The visitor centre at Burnham Beeches has a café serving sandwiches and cakes; it is open every day except Christmas Day, but there is no indoor seating. The centre has a display about the history and wildlife of the woods, and there are public toilets. Tel. 01753 647358.

THE WALK

1. From the visitor centre walk back along Lord Mayor's Drive for about 230 yards, ignoring small paths on the left. Take a major path on the left. This is recognizable because, at the time of writing, it has a rubbish bin and 'Walkers only' sign at the start and lies where the trees end and an open area starts. Follow the path down into a dip, across The Nile, and up the other side to a cross-path.

The Nile is one of two streams found in Burnham Beeches. This part of the woods is called Egypt because gypsies used to camp round here,

93

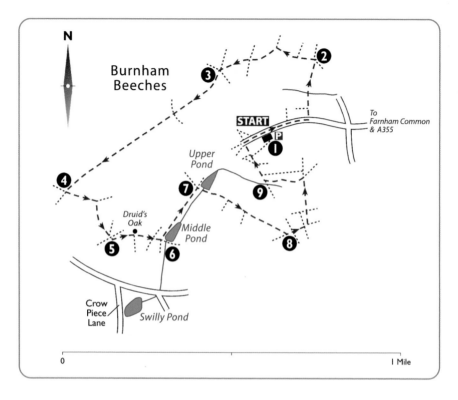

and I suppose that is how the stream got its name. A short way
downstream the water disappears at a series of swilly or swallow holes.
These occur at the point where impermeable clay on the surface meets
permeable chalk and the water sinks into the ground. The swilly holes
are close to the footbridge mentioned at point 3, below but are hardly
discernible.

2. Turn left. Keep ahead on this path, ignoring all paths to the right,
eventually going downhill again to a complex path junction.

3. Bear slightly left – *not* the path sharp left that leads down to a
footbridge. Cross a surfaced drive and continue ahead on Victoria
Drive for about 700 yards. If you reach a road you have gone about 250
yards too far.

4. At a major cross-path turn left uphill. At a fence at the top of the hill,
turn right to emerge on a surfaced drive by a gate.

5. Go through the gate, cross the drive, and take a path to the right of the drive that leads to Middle Pond.

Growing in the open space to the left of the path is what is reputed to be the most ancient tree in the Beeches, an ancient bulk called the Druids Oak. There is no historical reason for this particular tree having that name; it is probably a bit of Victorian whimsy. It is surrounded by a protective fence and appears to be on its last legs, but has apparently looked much the same for the last century. You may also have observed that many of the older trees are huge and have a very gnarled and weird appearance. This is because nearly all the old beeches have been pollarded in the past. Pollarding is an old form of dual-purpose woodland management. The trees were regularly lopped at head height to provide fuel, and wood for small building jobs. The trees have the capacity to sprout new branches and can be cut on a twelve to fifteen year rotation. Lopping them at head height keeps the succulent new growth safe from the animals that were allowed to graze the forest floor beneath. A beech tree would ordinarily live for about 250 years, but this apparently brutal practice allows the tree to live for 400 years or more and grow into the gnarled giants for which Burnham Beeches is famous.

6. Turn left to walk with the pond on the right. At the end of the pond continue by the stream, which may be dry, to a second pond, Upper Pond.

The stream flows down to an impressive swallow hole, called Swilly Pond. Unfortunately, there is no path leading to it, but it can be viewed from one of the roads. If you wish to see it, the best plan is to drive to Crow Piece Lane, shown on the map. I have seen it full of water about 50 yards across and hardly recognizable as a pond, depending on the state of the ground water.

7. Turn right across the end of Upper Pond and follow the path, soon crossing a more open area, to a T-junction with a cross-path.

8. Turn left, shortly crossing a surfaced drive. Some 100 yards after the drive, cross a path and, after a further 10 yards, turn left on a second path. After 50 yards continue ahead on a boardwalk for 100 yards; then turn left on a narrower boardwalk, across The Mire. (The boardwalk across The Mire is closed at certain times of year to protect the animals

(Main picture) Swilly Pond when full; (inset) Swilly Pond when empty

that live there from disturbance. In that case, continue ahead for about 60 yards and then, at the end of the boardwalk, go through a gate and immediately turn left to follow a path to the surfaced drive a bit further on.)

The Mire is a boggy area fed by the same stream that has been dammed to create the ponds and is home to many plants that thrive in these conditions.

9. At the end of the boardwalk turn right along a surfaced drive. At a cross drive turn right, back to the visitor centre.